simple
winning
chess

by Chris Baker

EVERYMAN CHESS

Everyman Chess, formerly Cadogan Chess, is published by Everyman Publishers, London

First published in 1999 by Everyman Publishers plc, formerly Cadogan Books plc, Gloucester Mansions, 140A Shaftesbury Avenue, London WC2H 8HD in association with Gambit Publications Ltd, 69 Masbro Road, London W14 0LS.

British Library Cataloguing in Publication Data
A CIP catalogue record for this book is available from the British Library.

ISBN 1 85744 225 3

Distributed in North America by The Globe Pequot Press, 6 Business Park Road, P.O. Box 833, Old Saybrook, Connecticut 06475-0833.
Telephone 1-800 243 0495 (toll free)

All other sales enquiries should be directed to Everyman Chess, Gloucester Mansions, 140A Shaftesbury Avenue, London WC2H 8HD
tel: 0171 539 7600 fax: 0171 379 4060

To my son, Thomas, and my partner, Mihaela.

EVERYMAN CHESS SERIES (formerly Cadogan Chess)
Chief Advisor: Garry Kasparov
Series Editor: Murray Chandler

Edited by Graham Burgess and typeset by John Nunn for Gambit Publications Ltd.

Printed in Great Britain by Redwood Books, Trowbridge, Wilts.

Contents

Symbols

+	check
++	double check
#	checkmate
x	capture
!!	brilliant move
!	good move
!?	interesting move
?!	dubious move
?	bad move
??	blunder
+−	White is winning
±	White has a large advantage
⩲	White is slightly better
=	the game is equal
⩱	Black is slightly better
∓	Black has a large advantage
−+	Black is winning
Ch	championship
Cht	team championship
Wch	world championship
Ct	candidates event
IZ	interzonal event
Z	zonal event
OL	olympiad
ECC	European Clubs Cup
jr	junior event
wom	women's event
mem	memorial event
rpd	rapidplay game
corr	correspondence game
qual	qualifying event
1-0	the game ends in a win for White
½-½	the game ends in a draw
0-1	the game ends in a win for Black
(n)	nth match game
(D)	see next diagram

Introduction

I have organized the topics in this book in the order in which we encounter them: before we start the game, during the game and after the game. Obviously some things are difficult to categorize exactly, but I feel that this presentation has worked well, and will help readers to come to grips with some important concepts.

The book itself should be of use to a wide range of players since it contains some quite 'meaty' games and analysis together with general advice, based on my many years of competitive play and teaching experience. This advice should help you to gain, or at least save, valuable points.

As it is such a new and rapidly-changing topic, not much has been written hitherto on the use of computer aides. I hope that the section on this will give plenty of food for thought to players considering purchasing and using the range of powerful software that is now available.

With the wealth of opening books now on the market, I felt it was appropriate to give advice to help ensure that the reader chooses the most appropriate opening repertoire for himself; in this way he will be able to spend money wisely on the material most suitable for his own needs.

I enjoyed constructing Chapter 16, Bolts from the Blue; I chose positions and moves that have sparked my imagination and motivated me when feeling stale. I am sure you will also enjoy Chapter 4, on blunders – although here we may be laughing at the expense of others, there are important lessons to be learnt too. The idea of writing a chapter on 'When to Offer a Draw' occurred to me since I couldn't remember the idea having been covered before and the importance of the topic should not be underestimated.

A lot of people have in the past asked me how they should develop and improve their game. My reply is invariably that before they go any further they should improve their technique, whether in the middlegame or endgame. Doing so can improving their results by 5-10% without altering their openings or style at all – if only all of our development could rely on something so non-traumatic!

The way in which people handle the clock never ceases to amaze me. Therefore I have written what may seem to be simply stating the obvious, but experience suggests that this advice needs to be repeated. As I tell the 7-8 year olds I coach, you wouldn't go into a three-hour maths exam and finish after 3 minutes or answer one question in $2^3/_4$ hours and expect to answer the last four adequately in the last fifteen minutes! Even more 'obvious' to myself was the section on how to behave at the board; having said that, as long as I sit there and some opponents behave the way they do, something should be said!

You may be wondering how to use this book to maximum advantage. I would advise readers to look through the book once, picking out general points and 'food for thought', making a note of the aspects of their own game that need the most attention and then read the relevant parts in detail, making notes on their 'course of action'. From this starting point they can maximize the benefit and move their own game forward accordingly. Having then decided on the best opening books for their own purposes and computer software to meet their requirements, they can take a close look at themselves in the mirror and decide how best to complete the 'cosmetic surgery' necessary to make themselves the player they want to be.

I remember as a young and relatively weak player setting myself various targets. These were:

1) To beat my brother (first but by no means least!);
2) Play for my country;
3) Get myself a title; and
4) Become world champion (well, I was young!).

More to the point I did something about it, by undergoing a regime to improve my own game. I remember vividly trying to improve my memory by:

1) Trying to play through my game on a board without using the scoresheet (and by using it as a prompt when I got stuck); and

2) Trying to play through my game by repeating it out in chess notation, or going through it in my head and using a set or my scoresheet as a prompt when I had problems. This habit led me on to the natural follow-up of discussing games/variations in the car, or on the train, with friends (quite often much stronger players) on the way to tournaments. Additionally, when I saw games with interesting ideas or moves in the opening that were within my own repertoire, I could remember the ideas and explore them in the comfort of my own home. I would then introduce the useful ideas into my own play.

As for the future, I haven't given up the hope of improving my own game further – there is still the grandmaster title to aim for! I must say that writing this book has given me some ideas that I intend to use myself with the sole purpose of developing my own game; maybe in that respect this book will turn out to be one of *my* better purchases!

Finally I would like to wish all my readers every success and '*bon chance*' with their improvement. After all, it is only with our own personal development that we can raise the general standard of chess and get closer to the 'truth' behind this most regal game.

Chris Baker
Bath 1999

Part 1: Before the Game

In this section I have presented what I view as the essential topics for players who wish to improve their results by being fully ready for their games. Failing to have a consistent and well-researched opening repertoire seems to me like going into an examination without having read the syllabus. Moreover, as I tell my students, it is just as essential not to give up on a system due to a couple of bad experiences. Instead, one should repair the damage by either improving on the existing line (see, for example, Baker-Dickenson on page 24) or adopting a similar variation by way of an alternative. In this way they don't become a 'jack of all trades and a master of none'.

The aspiring player needs to develop the habit of looking at positions that arise in variations he plays and an ability to seek out ideas that improve on known 'theory' (see Topalov-Van Wely on page 38 for a good example). People like Kasparov have a team working full-time on developing such ideas and keeping these 'secrets' for the appropriate moment.

Developing your middlegame requires time and persistence in playing through ideas that commonly occur, especially in the openings you play. When playing through these games you should developing an understanding of the position and its themes, since you can try to use these ideas in your own games.

As far as endgame technique is concerned, I believe that only laziness can account for people not bringing their game up to scratch on basic situations that can be logically determined, e.g. basic rook and pawn endings, etc. I know my knowledge has gained me many a point over the years as my opponents have got it wrong. Having said that, you obviously need a good reference book to learn from in the first place!

Good self-discipline is needed to reduce the number of blunders you make. In Chapter 4 I have provided some simple methods that should help you to acquire this discipline.

Chapters 5 and 6 address the question of how to face opponents who are much stronger or weaker than yourself. The right approach and an understanding of the psychological elements of these situations can pay great dividends.

1 Opening Preparation

In the Beginning

To start off with, most children, after learning the rules of the game and the fundamental values of the pieces, play any and every opening move and defence. Therefore they obtain no consistency nor do they form any opening repertoire. If you asked them why they played, for instance, 1...e6 against 1 e4 they would probably reply 'I dunno' or 'I just felt like it'.

They then move on slightly when a friend shows them 'Fool's Mate' and they play it as White at every opportunity, scoring some very quick wins. Winning so quickly even helps them ignore the games against slightly better children where they obtain a bad position or lose hopelessly, but it takes twenty or thirty moves to happen. At this stage they do little in the way of real analysis and the emphasis is more on bashing out moves at a great rate of knots, many of their games starting 1 e4 e5 2 ♕h5 g6 3 ♕xe5+ and 4 ♕xh8 or 1 e4 e5 2 ♕h5 ♘c6 3 ♗c4 ♘f6 4 ♕xf7#. The game of chess seems so easy! They cannot wait for their friends to finish so that they can boast about how they got their opponent in Fool's Mate in four moves and twenty seconds.

Things then develop as somebody, quite often an adult, shows them how to stop their opponent playing Fool's Mate and achieve an advantage, even as Black, from an early stage by gaining time on their opponent's queen with well-timed minor-piece play. This aides them to reach the next stage of maturity but leaves them with the question of what to do as White themselves instead of their accustomed 1 e4, 2 ♕h5, etc. For a while, at least 95% of their games as White or Black will still start 1 e4 e5. Some of the more talented or those with a more mature attitude will then develop and earn respect from their peers within the school or in local junior tournaments. They show a keen interest in the game and are hungry for more. Some may receive group coaching from a school master or even attend group coaching sessions by a local league player. This still leaves a void as in group coaching, with the best will in the world, it is difficult for the coach to recognize individual styles or spend too much time on specific opening theory. One or two books might be recommended and maybe at a local club an experienced player will play an odd game or two and recommend an opening or defence.

However, there is still a big gap to breach between school and league chess. It can be very disheartening for a child who has some confidence and self-belief to go along to a chess club only to be set up with a couple of 'friendly' games (there's no such thing!), lose dismally and to go away again. His reaction may be one of 'Oh, I'm rubbish at chess really; I'll spend my time doing something else instead'. Sometimes the club environment can be at first a little hostile or the club may not even be very 'junior-friendly'. It may even be that the child turns up on a night when there is a match, and he doesn't get a game or any real attention at all. Clubs must take some of the blame for this and should make an effort as it is imperative to encourage these young minds since it is these people who, as they develop, will replace the players who leave league chess for whatever reason.

I know at my old club (Keynsham, which has teams in the Bristol League and the Somerset League) a real effort was made by Sebastian Buckley and David Woodruff to spend time with all new members and in particular juniors to make them feel at home, comfortable and welcome. The club even went as far as deliberately running a team in the lowest division of the local league specifically for less experienced players and newcomers. The idea is that as people developed they could move up to a team in a higher division (one advantage of a larger club) and make way for other newcomers, although as many people as possible were to be given a chance to play in the lowest side rather than always the 'best team' being picked. On more than one

occasion in the past when I have gone to the club Sebastian has sat me down against a young player and told me to have a game, sometimes removing both my rooks (and sometimes my queen as well!). There are a couple of these children now (James McArthur and Chris Haydon) that I'd rather not give odds to at all!

During this stage, juniors start to play openings and defences more consistently but still have little in the way of theory that they can digest properly. Moreover, the openings they play are influenced by stronger players around them or somebody who has taken them under their wing. These people, while experienced, are, with the greatest respect, possibly not very strong players or professional coaches. I make this comment 'with the greatest respect' carefully and with gratitude as without them many children would not get this 'in-between' help they desperately need. The result though is that the child gets to form an opening repertoire based on these influences. Quite naturally, they will more often than not be taught what these players play themselves. This is fair enough as this is what they understand themselves.

This is the stage where the influence of a professional coach/player is extremely useful. If for nothing else, he can get to know the child, his strengths and weaknesses and what type of player he is becoming and what style he is developing. A great deal of thought and consultation can be given with the aim of forming a complete repertoire that will stand the player in good stead for the coming years. The coach can recommend books that are well written and pitched at the right level, together with giving advice on computer software and the quantity and quality of chess the child should be seeking.

When the child should make the 'jump' to adult league chess or from minor to major tournaments, etc., is a big decision and a topic we will look at in depth in another part of this book. Having formed an opening repertoire, he should try to get as much practice as possible with it in 'friendlies', games against a computer or in less important matches prior to playing it in 'serious' or in more important games. This helps to build confidence and acquire further understanding.

There is a big temptation here for the child to lose a game and state that the French, for example, is rubbish and the secret to all of his problems is to play the answer to the secret of the universe, the Sicilian Dragon. While I won't (and cannot) say one main line defence is better than another (this is like saying blue cars are better than red, which in turn are better than yellow) as they are just a matter of taste and suitability. The important thing following a loss (especially a painful one) is to patch up the line played, learn from the mistake, whether it was a strategic or tactical one and therefore increase one's understanding of the opening in question. The decision to change an opening you play should only be taken with careful thought and

consideration. Hopping from one line to another is just an easy 'get-out' and will lead to confusion, frustration and impede further development.

The Good, the Bad and the Ugly

Moving on, we see even quite talented, strong juniors and experienced adults having moments of confidence crisis. Recently I travelled with the Welsh teams to Holland for the annual Glorney and Faber Cup events. Warning bells should have already struck when a parent of one of the players phoned me the evening before we were due to leave, asking if I had any theory available on the Sicilian Dragon. It didn't register at the time that this was not something that he normally played and, besides, I always welcome any involvement from the children or parents involved in coaching I do in regard to preparation for games or tournaments.

Before I go further with this story, I should make it clear I am in no way blaming the boy concerned for what happened – more just recognizing it as a natural progression of previous circumstances. He had received formal coaching by an experienced grandmaster who had done a very good job of both training him and building up a sensible and reliable opening repertoire. This had stopped some time before the event concerned as the grandmaster involved had moved to a different area. This left the boy with a void which couldn't be readily filled due to the remoteness of his locality. As time went on and the boy played stronger and stronger opposition due to his progression as a player, cracks appeared in his openings that could and should have been plugged. Instead, doubts started to develop in his mind, thoughts that his repertoire was inadequate, and, as often is the case, that anybody and everybody that he was going to play knew everything about the opening he was playing (or at least knew which variations would cause him the most problems). This snowballs as the person involved is then convinced that every opponent is bound to play the very variation that concerns him the most.

When there is some kind of irrational fear in a player's mind before he even sits down to play, there is a problem. Returning to the event concerned, after we arrived in Holland I spoke to the player at length and explained that although his choice of going from the Sicilian Accelerated Dragon to Dragon main lines to avoid, in particular, the Maroczy Bind was a sound one, it had immediate drawbacks. Firstly, after 1 e4 c5 2 ♘f3 instead of 2...♘c6 he would need to play 2...d6. Against this move, there are various alternative anti-Sicilian lines he needed to be prepared for, but secondly, and of far greater concern, was the vast amount of theory involved in playing the main-line Dragon. Unlike some opening variations, the Dragon is not something you should even attempt to play 'off the cuff'. I suggested that the best

option was to stick with what he knew and on his return from the event to do some serious work on the Dragon. This would involve playing through some lines, preferably with someone of his own strength (or better), playing lots of friendlies – five minute games to get into the swing of it – and then try it out in some matches of lesser importance. Unfortunately, no games may seem of 'lesser importance' but local league games or a weekend tournament, which you can afford to put down to experience, may be the best bet. Then, as confidence and experience grows, in particular in the recurrent themes of the variation chosen, introduce the defence (if possible) against the most suitable opposition. In this way the introduction of a new opening/variation can be achieved in the least painful way. Often initial results with it can be very good as your confidence in your new 'pet line' is high and playing something new can get you out of a rut and also be refreshing due to the new ideas. This seemed to make sense to him and perhaps the story would have ended there if that is how things had progressed.

Maybe this is also a good point for me to accept some of (or even a large proportion of) the blame. Whereas I continued with preparing the players the best I could, with them having the very busy schedule of two rounds a day, by giving them print-outs of opponents' games for the colours they were due and looking at variations with some of the squad where I thought it would be of use, I failed to put enough work into their psychological state (or at least I failed with the player in question). What happened next was quite logical in an illogical way. The player concerned was due to have Black against one of the stronger sides and decided, after talking to another member of the squad (who offered the advice with the best of intentions), to play the Caro-Kann as a safe and solid way of meeting 1 e4. This of course in itself is quite true, although White still has a wide range of options to liven things up and also has a number of different set-ups he can aim for to try to claim an edge for White. The result, as shall see, was quite disastrous:

1 e4 c6 2 d4 d5 3 ♘c3 dxe4 4 ♘xe4 ♘d7

Perhaps a 'safer' variation to play would have been 4...♗f5 as after 5 ♘g3 ♗g6 6 ♘f3 ♘d7 7 h4 h6, etc., it is hard for White to do anything too startling, although 6 ♘1e2 might have caught Black by surprise given his lack of experience with the Caro.

5 ♗c4

This turns out to be a good choice. 5 ♘f3, while on paper about as strong, would have been less likely, at least in the short term, to have caused a major debacle, as Black achieves a solid position after 5...♘gf6 6 ♘xf6+ ♘xf6. Even here, though, there is some danger, as 7 ♘e5 needs to be met precisely.

5...♘gf6 6 ♘g5 e6 7 ♕e2 ♘b6 8 ♗d3 ♕xd4?! *(D)*

This is risky. His opponent after the game stated that this lost outright and in his state of mind at the time Black

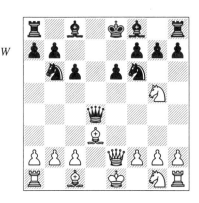

accepted this assessment without further thought. In fact this assessment is too blasé and if Black had prepared the capture on d4 as a surprise weapon, maybe things would have been different. 8...♕xd4?! has only been played very rarely at master level, and was an idea, not surprisingly, that Fritz came up with when I was doing work on the variation for my previous book, *A Startling Chess Opening Repertoire*. Play differs completely from the normal strategically and tactically solid Caro lines, and this may be one reason why people have given this possibility little attention.

9 ♘1f3 ♗b4+?

But this move shows Black's lack of understanding of the position at hand. 9...♕d5 10 ♘e5 ♕xg2 11 ♖f1 ♗e7 12 ♘ef3! seems critical and is the real test of 8...♕xd4?!.

10 c3! ♗xc3+ 11 ♔f1!

Black is, for all intents and purposes, busted.

Our player felt very guilty after the game and I must admit that my initial reaction was one of wondering why on earth he had played this opening, never mind 8...♕xd4?!. However, after this my next reaction was to feel very sorry for him. This was a very painful experience for him and a hard way to learn the lesson. It is also a strange phenomenon that whereas a player thinks that his opponent has complete and utter knowledge of the opening line that he would normally play, he expects that the same opponent would know as little as he does when he plays something new and is unprepared.

Pre-game Preparation

Having looked at a bad experience when something was tried when ill-prepared, we should look at the opposite side of the coin. The following example is one of my own from the Hastings Challengers 1997/8. I was particularly pleased with it as my opponent, an experienced grandmaster, had proved to be an awkward opponent for me in the past and so I was happy to draw so comfortably as Black having been under no pressure. It is also very important to understand prior to looking at the game itself that most of the hard work was before even sitting down to play the game.

McNab – Baker
Hastings Challengers 1997/8

1 c4 e5 2 ♘c3 ♘f6 3 ♘f3 ♘c6 4 e4

When examining Colin's games from my databases, this slightly unusual fourth move caught my eye. I noticed further that after Black's reply

he had had the variation as far as his ninth move on more than one occasion.

4...♗c5 5 ♘xe5 ♘xe5

Black should avoid 5...♗xf2+ 6 ♔xf2 ♘xe5 7 d4 ± and 5...0-0 6 ♘f3! ♖e8 7 d3 ± Nimzowitsch-Yates, Dresden 1926.

6 d4 ♗b4

6...♘xe4 7 ♘xe4 ♗b4+ 8 ♘c3 ±.

7 dxe5 ♘xe4 8 ♕d4

8 ♕f3 ♘xc3 9 bxc3 ♗a5 10 ♗a3 d6 11 exd6 0-0 was unclear in Rohde-Dlugy, New York 1990.

8...♘xc3 9 bxc3 (D)

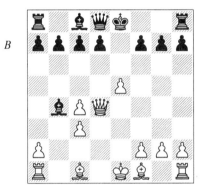

9...c5!?

The stem game for this move was Petzold-Molinaroli, 2nd Bundesliga 1995/6. Other moves are more popular though, but illustrate some of the potential problems for Black, viz. 9...♗e7 (9...♗a5 10 ♗a3 d6 11 0-0-0 0-0 12 exd6 cxd6 13 ♕xd6 ♕xd6 14 ♗xd6 ± Korchnoi-Hübner, Solingen 1973) 10 ♕g4 and now:

a) 10...♔f8 11 ♕g3!? d6 12 ♗e3 dxe5 13 ♖d1 and now either 13...♕e8

14 ♕xe5 ♗d6 15 ♕h5 ± or 13...♗d7 14 ♗e2 ±.

b) 10...g6 11 ♗h6 d6 12 ♕e4! (12 ♕f4 dxe5 13 ♕xe5 f6 14 ♕e3 ♔f7 and 12 ♕g3 ♗e6 13 ♗e2 ♕d7 are both unclear) 12...♕d7 (12...♗f5 13 ♕xb7 ♖b8 14 ♕xa7 ±; 12...dxe5 13 ♖d1 ±) 13 ♗d3 (13 ♖d1 ♕f5 14 ♗d3 ♕xe5 15 ♕xe5 dxe5 16 ♗g7 ♖g8 17 ♗xe5 c6 18 0-0 ♗e6 is unclear) 13...dxe5 (13...♕f5 14 exd6 ♕xe4+ 15 ♗xe4 cxd6 16 0-0 ±) 14 0-0 (14 ♗g7!? ♖g8 15 ♗xe5 f5! 16 ♕e3 ♕c6 17 0-0 ♗e6 18 ♖fe1 gives White an attack) 14 ♕xe5 ♕e6 15 ♗f4 (15 ♗g7 ♖g8 16 0-0 f6 17 ♕xe6 ♗xe6 ∓) 15...f6 16 ♕xe6 ♗xe6 17 ♗xc7 ♖c8 18 ♗g3 ♗xc4 ∓) 14...f6 15 f4 ♕c6 and White has the initiative after 16 ♕xc6+ bxc6 17 fxe5, as in Conquest-Khalifman, Hastings 1995/6.

10 ♕e3

Previously only 10 ♕d3 had been played, when I think the game offers balanced chances.

10...♗a5 11 ♗d2?!

More to the point is 11 ♗a3, provoking the advance 11...b6. White can then hope that with the pawn on b6, Black's dark-squared bishop may become locked out of the game. I remember looking at lines where White tried to follow this up with a later ♖ad1-d6. Even in these lines, though, Black is not without chances. Obviously though, one of the benefits of introducing a move such as 9...c5!? is that it puts the opponent on his own resources over the board. Moreover, he may by now be smelling a rat and treat with distrust something that otherwise

he may regard as natural. Psychology is a wonderful thing when it works in your favour!

11...♕e7 12 ♗d3 d6!

12...♗c7 is an alternative which would keep more tension and perhaps offer Black decent chances. The textmove, though, is strong as it soon liquidates to a position where White must be very careful not to over-stretch.

13 exd6 ♕xe3+ 14 fxe3 ♗e6 15 e4 0-0-0 16 e5 f6!

This is the key move to follow up 12...d6. It is obviously imperative for Black to break open the centre before White can consolidate his position.

17 0-0-0!

A well-judged move. Alternatives would leave White on the point of no return. Colin, as befits a strong player, finds just the right time to accept things haven't gone right and to bale out to a draw.

17...fxe5 18 ♖he1 ♖xd6 19 ♖xe5 ♖xd3 ½-½

After 20 ♖xc5+ ♗c7 21 ♖xc7+ ♔xc7 22 ♗f4+ ♔c8 23 ♖xd3 ♗xc4 things have petered out.

I cannot overstate the pleasurable feeling one gets upon achieving a good result against a stronger opponent or the confidence you can feel when after a few moves your opponent is way down on the clock, sitting at the board working hard and you know you have had that same position on your board at home that morning or the previous evening. If Colin had known what I had in store for him, he would have had the choice between playing a different variation or preparing it further himself. Although I think it would have been hard to predict 9...c5!?, another important point is that 9...c5!? not only avoided the majority of known theory but also maintained tension in the position.

Coincidentally, a game Knott-Gormally was being played only three boards away from me at Hastings and continued 9...♗e7, soon petering out to a draw. While Black was never in real trouble, he didn't have any realistic chances to play for an initiative either. I should point out that I'm in no way trying to say that Simon Knott is a 'bunny' (in fact he is an experienced FM who has taken some decent scalps in the past), but I would expect that someone of Danny Gormally's class would be aiming to play for more.

Opening Secrets

Most strong players have ideas or lines saved away to play against the right player at the right time. One famous example is when Marshall introduced an early form of what is now known as the Marshall Attack.

Capablanca – Marshall
New York 1918

1 e4 e5 2 ♘f3 ♘c6 3 ♗b5 a6 4 ♗a4 ♘f6 5 0-0 ♗e7 6 ♖e1 b5 7 ♗b3 0-0 8 c3 d5 9 exd5 ♘xd5 10 ♘xe5 ♘xe5 11 ♖xe5 ♘f6 (D)

Nowadays 11...c6 is played almost without hesitation although alternatives such as the text-move or 9...e4?! (the Herman Steiner Variation) are

used occasionally, often for their surprise value. Marshall had apparently been 'saving' 8...d5 for some years ready to play against Capablanca! In this case the story had a sad ending, with Capablanca virtually refuting 11...♘f6 over the board! In a way it's a shame that the Marshall Attack didn't receive a better fate on its first outing although it is amazingly impressive to me how Capablanca both kept his cool and side-stepped all of the possible minefields during the game.

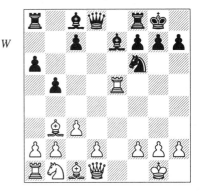

12 ♖e1 ♗d6 13 h3 ♘g4 14 ♕f3 ♕h4 15 d4

Avoiding 15 hxg4 ♗h2+! 16 ♔f1 ♗xg4 17 ♕e4 ♗f4! 18 g3 ♕h2 19 ♖e3 (Black wins after 19 ♗xf7+ ♔xf7 20 ♕d5+ ♔g6 21 ♖e6+ ♗xe6 22 ♕xe6+ ♔h5 23 ♕d5+ ♗g5 24 ♕g2 ♖xf2+ 25 ♕xf2 ♕h1+ 26 ♔e2 ♖e8+) 19...♖ae8 20 ♕d5 ♗xg3! 21 ♖xg3 (21 ♕xf7+ ♔h8!) 21...♖e2+ 22 ♔e1 ♗f3+ and Black wins.

15...♘xf2 16 ♖e2

It was later established that 16 ♗d2! is more convincing. 16...♗b7

(16...♗e6?! 17 ♕xf2 ♗g3 18 ♕e3 ♗xe1 19 ♗xe1 ±) 17 ♕xb7 ♘d3 18 ♖e2 and now:

a) 18...♖ae8 19 ♕f3 ♖xe2 20 ♕xe2 ♕g3 21 ♕f3! ♕h2+ 22 ♔f1 ♕h1+ 23 ♔e2 ♘xb2 24 ♗e3 +–.

b) 18...♕g3 19 ♔f1! ♘f4 (19...♕h2 20 g4! ♕xh3+ 21 ♕g2 ♕h4 22 ♗e3 ♖ae8 23 ♘d2 ♗f4 24 ♘f3 ♕h6 25 ♗c2 +–) 20 ♖f2! ♕d3+ 21 ♔g1 ♘e2+ 22 ♖xe2 ♕xe2 23 ♕f3 ♕xf3 24 gxf3 ±.

16...♗g4 17 hxg4

Not 17 ♕xf2? ♗g3 18 ♕f1 ♗xe2 19 ♕xe2 ♖ae8 –+.

17...♗h2+ 18 ♔f1 ♗g3 19 ♖xf2 ♕h1+ 20 ♔e2 ♗xf2 21 ♗d2 ♗h4 22 ♕h3 ♖ae8+ 23 ♔d3 ♕f1+ 24 ♔c2 ♗f2 25 ♕f3 ♕g1 26 ♗d5 c5 27 dxc5 ♗xc5 28 b4 ♗d6 29 a4 a5 30 axb5 axb4 31 ♖a6 bxc3 32 ♘xc3 ♗b4 33 b6 ♗xc3 34 ♗xc3 h6 35 b7 ♖e3 36 ♗xf7+ 1-0

Black will be mated after 36...♖xf7 (36...♔h7 37 ♕f5+ ♔h8 38 ♖xh6#) 37 b8♕+ ♔h7 38 ♖xh6+ ♔xh6 (or 38...gxh6 39 ♕xf7#) 39 ♕h8+ ♔g6 40 ♕h5#.

Another amazing example of a theoretical novelty (TN) was prepared and used at the highest level in the second Kasparov-Karpov world championship match.

Karpov – Kasparov
Moscow Wch (16) 1985

1 e4 c5 2 ♘f3 e6 3 d4 cxd4 4 ♘xd4 ♘c6 5 ♘b5 d6 6 c4 ♘f6 7 ♘1c3 a6 8 ♘a3 *(D)*

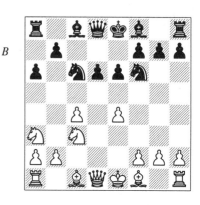

This position has been reached thousands of times before in high-level games, including Karpov-Kasparov, Moscow Wch (3) 1984/5. Then Kasparov played the normal and accepted move 8...♗e7. In the 1985 rematch he introduced the text-move, firstly in game twelve (see the note to White's eleventh move) and then in this, the sixteenth game.

8...d5!?
Strictly speaking this wasn't totally new as it had been played before in Honfi-Dely, Hungarian Ch 1965. No doubt Kasparov and his analytical team had prepared this variation thoroughly, anticipating that the resulting positions would suit Kasparov better than Karpov, as opposed to 8...♗e7, which tends to lead to long positional struggles where White can maintain a long-term spatial advantage together with a certain amount of control of the position (very much Karpov's forte). After 8...d5!? White can win a pawn (and must attempt to if he is to prove any kind of real opening advantage) but must concede a certain amount of

freedom/positional pressure as compensation.

9 cxd5

Karpov's little joke, although reversing the pawn captures (Game 12 had gone 9 exd5 exd5 10 cxd5 ♘b4) doesn't affect things in any way.

9...exd5 10 exd5 ♘b4 11 ♗e2

Game 12 of the same match went 11 ♗c4 (in the stem game, Honfi-Dely, Hungarian Ch 1965, White played 11 ♕a4+ but didn't prove any real advantage) 11...♗g4 12 ♗e2 ♗xe2 13 ♕xe2+ ♕e7 14 ♗e3 ♘bxd5 15 ♘c2 ♘xe3 16 ♘xe3 ♕e6 17 0-0 ♗c5 18 ♖fe1 0-0 ½-½. It is typical for Karpov, when faced by something unusual, to 'chicken out', with the idea of going back to the drawing board with his team with the objective of finding the weakness of the system in case it should be repeated. In the 14th game of the match, Karpov had side-stepped the whole line, but now he evidently felt he was ready.

11...♗c5?!

Apparently this came as a shock to Karpov and his team. They had only considered Black regaining the pawn here, when they thought that White could maintain a pleasant edge with a timely ♗f3.

The reason for the 'dubious' marking for this move and White's reply will be explained at the end of the game.

12 0-0?! 0-0 13 ♗f3

Maybe White should have 'bottled out' with 13 ♗g5 ♘bxd5 14 ♘xd5 ♕xd5 15 ♗xf6 ♕xd1 16 ♖fxd1 gxf6 with a likely draw. However, Karpov

had already 'wasted' one White and had come to this game ready to punish Black for repeating the gambit.

13...♗f5 14 ♗g5

14 ♗e3 is an alternative but after 14...♗xe3 15 fxe3 ♕b6 16 ♕d2 (16 ♘c4 ♕c5 17 ♕d4 ♕xd4 18 exd4 ♗d3 19 ♘b6 ♗xf1 20 ♘xa8 ♗xg2! is unclear) 16...♖fe8 the e3-pawn becomes a target.

14...♖e8!

It is essential to control the e4-square, as 14...b5? 15 ♗e4! would have shown.

15 ♕d2

15 ♘c4!?, again with the idea of returning the pawn, was possible but unlikely to offer anything special after 15...♗d3 16 a3 ♗xc4 (16...♗xf1? 17 axb4 ♗xc4 18 bxc5 is better for White) 17 axb4 ♗xb4 18 ♖e1 (18 ♕d4? ♗xf1 19 ♕xb4 ♗b5!) 18...♖xe1+ 19 ♕xe1 with chances for both sides.

15...b5 16 ♖ad1

White could have considered 16 ♕f4 ♗g6 17 ♗xf6 ♕xf6 18 ♕xf6 or 16 d6 ♖a7 17 ♖ad1 although in both cases Black is doing fine.

16...♘d3! 17 ♘ab1?

17 ♗e2? is no better, as 17...♘xf2! 18 ♖xf2 b4 shows. 17 d6 was necessary, when amongst others Black could try the exchange sacrifice 17...♕xd6!? 18 ♗xa8 ♖xa8 (18...♘g4? 19 ♗f4!) and now, with ...♘g4 a threat, Black has the initiative.

17...h6 18 ♗h4 b4! *(D)*

Forcing the knight to the edge as now 19 ♘e2 g5! (19...♘e5 20 ♘d4! is unclear) 20 ♗xg5 ♘xf2 21 ♖xf2 (21 ♗xf6 ♘e4+!) 21...♗xf2+ 22 ♔xf2 hxg5 23 ♕xg5+ ♗g6 would be good for Black.

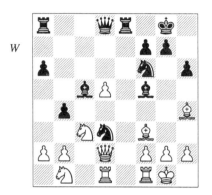

19 ♘a4 ♗d6 20 ♗g3 ♖c8 21 b3 g5!!

This move seems at first sight anti-positional, as it voluntarily weakens Black's kingside. However, Kasparov is in fact making full use of the resources in the position to maintain his 'monster' of a knight on d3.

22 ♗xd6

The natural 22 ♘b2, redeveloping the piece, falls into 22...♘xb2 23 ♕xb2 g4, while the alternative method to challenge the d3-knight by 22 ♗e2 is met by 22...♘e4!.

22 h4 may have been a good try, hoping for 22...g4? 23 ♗e2 ♘e4 24 ♕xh6! ♗f8 25 ♕h5 ♘xg3 26 fxg3 ♗g6 27 ♕xg4 ♖e4 28 ♕f3 ♘e5 29 ♕f2 ♗h6! (threatening ...♖c2) 30 ♘d2! ♗e3 31 ♘xe4 ♗xf2+ 32 ♘xf2 with excellent compensation for the queen. However, Black can obtain a promising position with 22...♘e4 or 22...♘f4!?.

22...♕xd6 23 g3

White would have liked to play 23 ♗e2 but after 23...♘f4 24 ♗c4 ♘g4 25 g3 ♖xc4! 26 bxc4 ♖e2 27 c5 (27 ♕d4 ♗e4) 27...♘h3+ 28 ♔g2 ♗e4+ 29 ♔xh3 ♕g6 he is getting mated.

23...♘d7!

Black uses some clever tactics to rule out White's last hope of playing ♘b2.

24 ♗g2

After 24 ♘b2 Black has the spectacular 24...♕f6!! 25 ♘xd3 (25 ♘c4 is more tenacious) 25...♗xd3 26 ♕xd3 (26 ♗g4 ♘e5! 27 f4 ♘xg4 28 ♕xd3 ♕b6+) 26...♘e5, when White's queen is trapped in broad daylight!

24...♕f6! 25 a3 a5 26 axb4 axb4 27 ♕a2 ♗g6! 28 d6

28 ♘d2 ♖e2! is decisive, while 28 ♗h3 is met by 28...♖cd8 threatening ...♘7e5.

28...g4! 29 ♕d2 ♔g7 30 f3

30 f4 ♗f5! is no better.

30...♕xd6 31 fxg4 ♕d4+ 32 ♔h1 ♘f6 33 ♖f4 ♘e4 34 ♕xd3 ♘f2+ 35 ♖xf2 ♗xd3 36 ♖fd2 ♕e3! 37 ♖xd3 ♖c1!! 38 ♘b2 ♕f2!

38...♖xd1+ 39 ♖xd1 ♕xb3 is also easily winning.

39 ♘d2 ♖xd1+

39...♖e2 mates one move more quickly!

40 ♘xd1 ♖e1+ 0-1

These annotations are partly based on those produced by Kasparov not long after the match concluded. Since then it has been found that 11...♘fxd5! is in fact best (as 11...♗c5?! 12 ♗e3! ♗xe3 13 ♕a4+ ♘d7 14 ♕xb4 ♗c5 15 ♕e4+ ♔f8 16 0-0 b5 17 ♘c2 favours White, Karpov-Van der Wiel, Brussels

1986), for example 12 0-0 ♗e6 13 ♘xd5 ♕xd5 14 ♗f3 ♕xd1 15 ♖xd1 ♗e7 16 ♗xb7 =. And so once more 11 ♗c4 ♗g4 becomes critical to the viability of the 'Kasparov Gambit'.

Whatever the final outcome of the theoretical discussion, it certainly did the damage at the time. Kasparov was by far the better prepared, while Karpov failed to solve the practical problems of the positions that arose.

Often ideas are produced at a much more modest level and therefore remain more or less 'hidden' unless 'spotted' and developed at home by a stronger player for future use. One of these 'secrets' came to light during a Glorney Cup game between Wales and Holland in 1997. In the following position Black came up with a surprise:

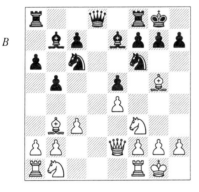

B

11...♘xe4!

This move wasn't mentioned as a possibility in the excellent (though now slightly dated) book by Tim Harding on the Marshall (and anti-Marshall lines).

12 ♕xe4

12 ♗xe7 ♘xe7 13 ♘xe5 occurred in the actual game although it appears to me as though Black has obtained comfortable equality.

12...♗xg5 13 ♗d5!

I thought at the time this was simply winning material due to the threat of 14 ♗xc6 as the c6-knight cannot be protected by the black queen due to his loose bishop on g5, e.g. 13...♕f6 14 ♘xg5 ♕xg5 15 ♗xc6 f5? 16 ♕d5+, etc.

13...♗f4!

At this point the rest of the Dutch team joined in the analysis with enthusiasm, suggesting ideas for both sides, showing their eagerness both to learn and to attempt to find the 'truth' about a position that had caught their imagination. This is a lesson in itself as it shows the kind of commitment young players should show in order to improve.

14 g3!

Necessary if White is intending to 'prove' an advantage.

14...♔h8!

This is the point. Black unpins his f-pawn and thus White is obliged to take the offered piece, but in return Black gets ferocious counterplay.

15 ♗xc6 f5 16 ♕e2 ♗xc6 17 gxf4 exf4

This is the critical position and one which you may wish to spend time analysing yourself. The conclusion I came to was that Black is doing very well and that White would find it very difficult (if not impossible) to develop and coordinate his pieces before falling foul of tactics along the h1-a8 diagonal or along the g-file. An obvious example of this would be 18 ♘bd2 ♖f6 19 ♔h1?? ♕xd2! 20 ♕xd2 ♗xf3+ 21 ♔g1 ♖g6#.

Finally in this section I would like to point out that even young and often comparatively weak players can come up with some interesting ideas. Perhaps they are helped by not being 'pre-conditioned' or because they lack the opening knowledge to know better! This surprising move arose in a recent Bristol Schools League match and I have to admit that when looking at the position with (ten-year-old) Christopher Garner I had to look twice before finding a solid enough (or simple enough) reason for him to accept that he shouldn't try it again against an unsuspecting opponent!

1 e4 e5 2 ♘f3 ♘c6 3 ♗c4 ♘f6 4 ♘g5 ♘xe4?! *(D)*

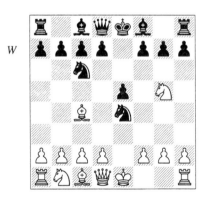

This surprising move is not simple to refute, and is based on the same idea

as 1 e4 e5 2 ♘f3 ♘c6 3 ♘c3 ♘f6 4 ♗c4 ♘xe4! 5 ♘xe4 d5, which I had gone through with some of the squad at the Paragon School in Bath.

5 ♘xf7

5 ♘xe4? d5 is fine for Black. After 5 ♗xf7+! ♔e7 I couldn't find anything totally convincing for White but I am reliably informed by John Nunn that Estrin's suggestion, 6 d4!, shatters Black's position.

5...♕f6

This was Garner's intended follow-up, but 5...♕h4 is a better move, and seems satisfactory for Black.

6 ♕e2!

The natural 6 0-0 may not be so clear after 6...♗c5! 7 ♕e2 (7 ♘xh8?! ♗xf2+ 8 ♖xf2 {not 8 ♔h1?? ♘g3+! and mate next move} 8...♕xf2+ 9 ♔h1 ♕d4 with an unclear position but one in which Black should be no worse) 7...♘xf2! 8 ♘xh8 (8 b4!? ♘xb4 9 ♘xh8 ♘xc2 seems to produce a fairly random position) 8...♘e4+ 9 d4 ♘xd4 and now:

a) 10 ♕h5+ g6 11 ♖xf6 gxh5 may well give Black the edge.

b) 10 ♖xf6 ♘xe2+ 11 ♔f1 ♘xc1 12 ♖f7 ♘d6 13 ♘c3! and White may be able to claim a small advantage.

6...♗c5

After 6...♘d6?! 7 ♘xh8 ♘d4 8 ♕d3 (8 ♕h5+ g6 9 ♕xh7 ♘xc2+ 10 ♔d1 ♘xa1 11 ♗d3 e4 12 ♖e1 is also strong for White) 8...♘xc4 9 ♕xc4 d5 10 ♕xc7 ♗d6 11 ♕f7+ ♕xf7 12 ♘xf7 ♔xf7 13 ♔d1 Black has insufficient compensation for the sacrificed material.

7 ♘xh8!

7 0-0 transposes to the note to White's 6th move, but 7 ♕xe4! ♕xf2+ 8 ♔d1 d5! 9 ♗xd5 ♗f5 10 ♕a4! is strong as well.

7...♗xf2+ 8 ♔d1

Black has insufficient counterplay. However, full marks to Chris for some creative thinking.

Next we will look at the following miniature, which shows what can go wrong if you try to 'make up' something new at the board rather than in pre-game preparation:

Baker – Beaumont
Bristol League 1997/8

1 d4 ♘f6 2 ♘f3 g6 3 ♘c3 ♗g7

Black avoids the Barry Attack (3...d5 4 ♗f4) and chooses to transpose instead to a Pirc. This was not unreasonable, as this was for many years his main defence to 1 e4.

4 e4 d6 5 h3

The drawback of this move-order is that I could no longer play my favourite Austrian Attack (in which White plays an early f4). I therefore chose a system which requires accurate and alert play by Black to avoid transposing to a Classical Pirc where White is a tempo ahead as he may play ♗f1-c4 in one move as opposed to ♗f1-e2 with a later ♗e2-c4 after the exchange of e-pawns.

5...c5?!

This experiment turns out badly. Better is 5...b6 with the idea of ...♗b7 putting pressure on the e4-pawn.

6 ♗b5+

This seems to me a logical and critical reply. Compared with the variation 1 e4 d6 2 d4 ♘f6 3 ♘c3 g6 4 f4 ♗g7 5 ♘f3 c5 6 ♗b5+, I am missing a pawn on f4 but the pawn on h3 is quite well placed, stopping any possibility of Black pinning the knight with ...♗g4 and also preparing the central thrust e4-e5 by taking g4 away from Black's f6-knight.

6...♘c6 7 dxc5! *(D)*

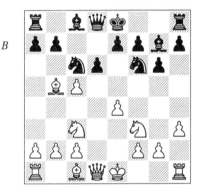

Black's standard method against the capture on c5 is to play ...♕a5 (threatening ...♘xe4) followed by ...♕xc5. However, here the presence of White's bishop on b5 prevents this.

7...♕a5 8 0-0 dxc5 9 ♘e5!

Thanks to the black king still being on e8, White is able to increase the pressure on c6.

9...♕b6?

9...♗d7, while not attractive, was probably Black's last chance to obtain some sort of reasonable position.

10 ♘c4 ♕c7 11 e5

An immediate 11 ♘d5 is not totally convincing in view of 11...♘xd5 12 exd5 a6 13 ♗xc6+ bxc6 14 d6! exd6 15 ♘xd6+ ♔f8 16 ♗e3.

11...♘d7 12 ♘d5 ♕d8

Following 12...♕b8 13 ♗f4 e6 (13...♘cxe5? 14 ♘xe5 ♗xe5 15 ♗xe5 ♕xe5 16 ♖e1 leaves Black with an appalling position) 14 ♘f6+ ♘xf6 (after 14...♗xf6 15 ♘d6+ ♔f8 16 exf6 Black is in dire straits) 15 exf6 ♕xf4 16 fxg7 ♖g8 17 ♖e1, Black has little chance of finding refuge, for example 17...♖xg7 18 ♘e5 f6 19 ♘xc6 ♗d7 20 ♘xa7! ♖xa7 21 ♕d5!.

13 ♗g5 ♘dxe5?

13...h6 is perhaps critical but after 14 ♘d6+ ♔f8 15 ♘xf7! ♔xf7 16 e6+ ♔xe6 (16...♔f8 17 ♗xc6 hxg5 18 ♗xd7 is not attractive) White has 17 ♘c7+!! ♕xc7 18 ♗c4+ ♔f5 19 ♕g4+ ♔e5 20 ♕f4#.

14 ♗xe7! 1-0

Since the black queen falls after 14...♕d7 15 ♘d6+.

Chris Beaumont is normally a well-prepared and technically very good player (only his addiction to time-trouble loses him valuable points) as the following TN shows. His reward was publication in the players 'bible', *Informator*. Only his failure to convert the position for the full point prevented him getting an even greater accolade.

Levitt – Beaumont
British League (4NCL) 1995/6

1 d4 ♘f6 2 c4 g6 3 ♘c3 ♗g7 4 e4 d6 5 f3 0-0 6 ♗e3

6 ♗g5 is another way of handling the white side.

6...c5 7 ♘ge2

Accepting the gambit by 7 dxc5 dxc5 8 ♕xd8 ♖xd8 9 ♗xc5 is considered to give Black adequate positional compensation.

7...♘c6 8 d5 ♘e5 9 ♘g3 e6 10 ♗e2 exd5 11 cxd5 a6

11...h5 has also been tried.

12 a4 ♗d7 13 f4?! ♘fg4!? *(D)*

This was the new move, leaving the black knight on e5 hanging. Previously 13...♘eg4 14 ♗d2 h5 15 h3 h4 16 hxg4 hxg3 was the main line, when 17 g5! was given by Joe Gallagher (improving over 17 e5?!), as advantageous for White.

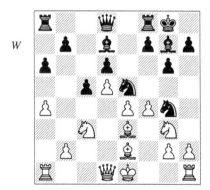

14 ♗g1

After 14 ♗f2? ♘xf2 15 ♔xf2 ♕f6! White has an unenviable position, e.g. 16 ♔e3?? ♕xf4+! 17 ♔xf4 ♗h6#, while after 14 ♗d2? ♕h4 15 fxe5 ♗xe5 all Black's pieces are working, while White has his king stuck in the centre. After 14 ♕d2 ♘xe3 15 ♕xe3 ♘g4 16 ♗xg4 ♗xg4 17 f5 ♕h4! 18 h3 (18 0-0?? loses the queen to 18...♗d4) 18...♗xf5 19 exf5 ♖ae8 20 ♘ce4,

20...gxf5! enables Black to regain the material with interest, while 20...♖xe4 21 ♕xe4 ♕xg3+ is also possible.

14...♕h4 15 fxe5

15 ♕d2 ♗h6 16 0-0-0 f5 leaves White tied up and facing a queenside attack after a future ...b5. The alternative 15 ♕c2 f5 16 0-0-0 ♗h6 again sees White facing serious problems.

15...♗xe5 16 ♗xg4

White could also try 16 ♗f2 ♘xf2 17 ♔xf2 f5 18 exf5 ♗xf5 19 ♗f3 g5 20 ♔e2 ♕c4+ 21 ♔d2 ♕d3+ 22 ♔e1 ♗xc3+ 23 bxc3 ♕xc3+ 24 ♔f2 g4, when Black comes out on top.

However, the critical line is 16 ♕d3 c4 17 ♕f3 f5 18 0-0-0 fxe4 19 ♕xe4 and now:

a) Not 19...♗xg3? 20 hxg3 ♕xh1 21 ♗xg4, when White has the advantage.

b) 19...♕g5+?! and here, rather than 20 ♔b1? ♗xg3 21 hxg3 ♗f5, winning for Black, as analysed by Levitt, White should play 20 ♖d2! ♗f4 21 ♕d4, which Nunn assesses as ±.

c) 19...♖f4, with unclear play, is considered best by Nunn.

16...♗xg3+!

16...♗xg4? 17 ♕d3 c4 18 ♕e3 f5 19 ♗f2! f4 20 ♘ge2! ♕xh2!? 21 ♕h3 lets White off the hook.

17 hxg3 ♕xh1 18 ♔f1

After 18 ♗xd7 ♕xg1+ 19 ♔d2 ♕xg2+ 20 ♕e2 ♕xg3 Black's material advantage should tell.

18...f5!

18...♗xg4? 19 ♕xg4 f5 20 ♕h3! fxe4+ 21 ♔e2 offers White good prospects of emerging with a reasonable position.

19 ♗f3 *(D)*

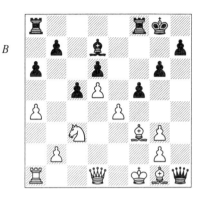

B

19...fxe4?

Finally, after all his good work, Black goes wrong. The correct continuation was 19...♖ae8! 20 ♕e2 (20 ♕c2 fxe4 21 ♘xe4 ♖xf3+ 22 gxf3 ♕xf3+ 23 ♘f2 ♗h3#) 20...fxe4 21 ♘xe4 ♗h3! 22 ♘f6+ (22 ♖a3 ♖xe4 finishes off) 22...♖xf6 23 ♕xe8+ ♖f8 24 ♕xf8+ (24 ♕e2 ♗xg2+ 25 ♕xg2 ♖xf3+ finally breaks White's resistance) 24...♔xf8 25 g4 h5! gives White huge problems.

20 ♘xe4 b5 21 b3 bxa4 22 bxa4 ♖ab8 23 ♘f2!

23 ♖a2 ♗f5 is unclear.

23...♕h6 24 ♕c1 ♕xc1+ 25 ♖xc1 ♗xa4 26 ♗h2! ♗b3 27 g4 ♖b6 28 g5 h6?!

Black misses his opportunity to maintain equality with 28...a5 29 ♘e4 ♗xd5! 30 ♘f6+ ♖xf6 31 gxf6 ♗xf3 32 gxf3 ♔f7 33 ♖d1.

29 gxh6 a5 30 ♖a1 a4 31 ♔e1 ♔h7 32 ♘e4?

The constant pressure finally takes its toll and White misses his chance for an advantage with 32 ♘g4! ♖a6 (32...♖f5 33 ♗g3 ♖a6 34 ♗h4 a3 35 ♗f6 ♗xd5 36 ♗xd5 ♖xd5 37 ♗g7) 33 ♔d2 a3 34 ♔c3 c4 35 ♗g1, when White has a definite plus.

32...♗xd5 33 ♘g5+ ♔xh6 34 ♗xd5 ♔xg5 35 ♖xa4 ♖f5 36 ♗e4 ♖f6 37 ♗g3 ♖e6 38 ♔d2 ½-½

As 38...♖b4 39 ♖xb4 cxb4 40 ♗d5 ♖f6 41 ♔c2 ♔g4 42 ♗h2 is equal.

A titanic struggle of the type that rarely occurs. A great deal of credit should also go to Jonathan Levitt for the sterling defence he came up with facing such an interesting novelty.

Finally I would like to show you a game which illustrates the point that after you lose a game with one of 'your' opening variations (pet lines) it is better to work on it, rebuild it and become stronger than to switch from opening to opening vaguely in the hope that you will find some sort of 'magical solution'.

Baker – Dickenson

British League (4NCL) 1998/9

1 e4 e6 2 ♘f3 d5 3 ♘c3 ♘f6 4 e5 ♘e4!?

An interesting idea that I originally came across with Fritz. One of its advantages is that it avoids a great deal of my preparation in the 'main lines'.

5 ♘e2 ♗c5!

Black provokes d2-d4, intending to 'lose' a tempo with his bishop. The benefit is that he no longer has to worry about his knight being kicked back by d2-d3.

6 d4 ♗e7 7 ♘g3 c5 8 ♗d3!

Previously I had played 8 dxc5 and lost horribly after trying to show I still 'had something' out of the opening against Simon Williams in the British League the previous season. It should have been obvious that I had something new (better!) in mind given that I was willing to repeat the variation. Then again perhaps my opponent wasn't aware of the history of the variation (but if not, he should have been, as these games are freely available on the Internet and elsewhere).

8...♘xg3 9 hxg3 cxd4 10 ♘xd4 ♕c7 11 ♕e2 ♗b4+? *(D)*

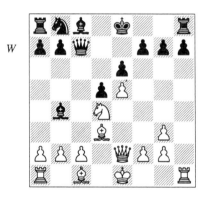

This is in principle wrong as it exchanges off White's 'bad' bishop while leaving Black with some bad long-term dark-square weaknesses as well as losing time (and time is money!).

12 ♗d2

I avoided 12 c3!! due to 12...♗xc3+ 13 bxc3 ♕xc3+ 14 ♕d2 ♕xa1, missing that 15 f4 is immensely strong for White due to the threat of 16 ♘b3 trapping the queen.

12...♗xd2+ 13 ♔xd2

White still has a pleasant position due to his lead in development, safer king and better bishop.

13...♘c6?!

Black's position is already close to collapse and so he tries to get White to commit his pieces in the hope it will work out badly.

14 ♘b5 ♕b6

I was expecting 14...♕a5+ 15 ♔c1 (I was worried that after 15 c3!? d4 Black could work up some counterplay against my king), when I feel that White is still better but there is still a lot of chess to be played.

15 ♖h4! *(D)*

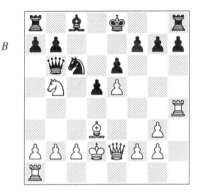

I liked this move as it protects the fourth rank while also threatening to swing along to the f- or g-file and offering the opportunity to double up on the h-file should it become relevant.

15...♗d7 16 ♖e1!

I wanted to discourage ...♘xe5 while bringing my last piece into the game.

16...♕a5+

16...♘xe5 17 ♕xe5 ♗xb5 18 ♕xg7 (I was trying to make 18 ♖b4 work but after 18...a6 19 a4 ♕xf2+ 20 ♖e2 ♕c5 White has nothing special) 18...0-0-0 19 ♗xb5 ♕xb5 20 ♕xf7 ♕xb2 21 ♕xe6+ ♔b8 22 ♕e5+ leads to a strong ending for White.

17 ♔d1! ♔e7?!

17...♔f8 was necessary although White still has a good position.

18 ♕e3!

Exploiting the dark-square weaknesses in Black's position.

18...h6?

18...♕xa2 19 ♕c5+ ♔d8 20 ♘d6 ♗e8 21 ♖b4! b6 (or 21...♘xb4? 22 ♘xb7+ ♔d7 23 ♗b5+ ♘c6 24 ♕xc6+ ♔e7 25 ♕d6#) 22 ♘xf7+ ♔c8 23 ♕d6! and Black's position falls apart.

19 ♕c5+ ♔d8 20 ♖f4 ♕xa2 21 ♖xf7 1-0

21...♕b1+ fails to 22 ♔d2 ♕xb2 23 ♖xd7+ ♔xd7 24 ♕d6+ ♔e8 25 ♗g6#.

This was especially pleasing as I was the only player in our team to win in a very tight four-all draw against a very strong Invicta Knights side.

Useful Tips

When you come across an interesting move in a line you play, whatever the source, make a note of it and the moves that lead up to it (or as sure as eggs are eggs you will not be able to remember them at a later stage) and then, 'back at the ranch', put in as much time as you can to find out all of the ins and outs of the move and its consequences. This is a useful exercise even if it is an idea for your opponent as then you are well prepared should it be played against you at a later date. If it is an idea for yourself, file it away carefully so that you can use it against a future opponent. This is best made use of if you find out prior to a game that he plays that particular line; then before the game itself you can refresh your memory by playing through your notes and lines of analysis.

These 'nest eggs' are especially useful if previously the line was thought to equalize for your opponent as Black (or offer them an advantage as White) as they are more readily going to enter the variation you desire. Finally, don't think that these ideas must be perfect – just that they are not obviously flawed and at least offer very good practical chances.

2 Middlegame Technique

Failing to convert a good position into victory is one of the most common weaknesses of inexperienced players. Sometimes it's a case of missing the winning plan but more often than not it's a case of failing to 'pick out' the best of many tempting moves. The position then 'drifts' from good or potentially very strong to unclear and the more experienced player seems to judge the situation better and come out on top. There is a temptation to expect the position to 'play itself' and also to avoid tactical possibilities that one would normally be happy to go into, on the (often unjustified) grounds that it should be unnecessary.

It is of vital importance to remain tactically sharp as this is a means of avoiding technical difficulties and making a quick, clean kill. One of the problems is that if you were to be set some tactical positions you would have an excellent chance of solving them as you would be 'made aware' that there is something specific to look for as opposed to having to remain vigilant move in move out. Moreover, you can't take back a move in a real game if it isn't the correct solution, nor play a few moves to see if it works out! For example, if I were to say to you that your house key, which you had lost, was under a cushion on the settee then you should have an excellent

chance, albeit after looking under a couple of other cushions first, of finding it. If, however, I were to tell you that some time during the next 4, 5 or 7 hours you would be within 'spitting distance' of that key, I wonder what your chance of finding it would be.

Let's first of all look at some positions where the player to move remained 'eagle-eyed'.

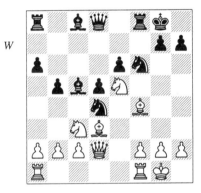

Baker – Spice
Cardiff 1998

Black had just played 13...b7-b5. There now followed:

14 ♗e3 ♕b6?

This natural and near-automatic response to White's move is also a logical follow-up to Black's previous move. However, there now comes a bombshell...

15 b4! ♗xb4 16 ♗xd4

Winning a piece as 16...♕xd4 loses the queen to 17 ♗xh7+. Not difficult in itself but a nice way to terminate what could otherwise have been a tense game.

The next example comes from the Oxford 1998 international tournament and although I suspect it may have well been a known opening trap, it still shows extreme vigilance from White, punishing Black mercilessly for his error.

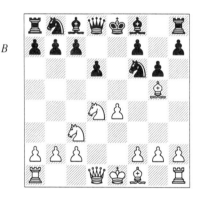

In this position Black played the casual...

6...h6?

Although this is a 'normal' type of move to gain time on the bishop, it is mistimed and is severely punished by White.

7 ♗xf6! ♕xf6 8 ♘d5 ♕d8 9 ♘b5 ♘a6 10 ♕d4!

Black is in deep trouble.

The next game shows inattentive play being punished.

R. O'Rourke – Baker
Bunratty 1999

1 e4 c5 2 ♘f3 ♘c6 3 d3 ♘f6 4 g3 d5 5 ♘bd2 g6 6 ♗g2 dxe4 7 dxe4 ♗g7 8 0-0 0-0 9 ♕e2?! *(D)*

Up to now I thought that we had played 'normal' moves but felt that I had achieved the semi-open type of position that would suit my style best. However, the text-move seems poorly timed. I would have expected 9 c3 first followed by a later ♕c2 or ♕e2, but perhaps White was worried about Black playing 9...♕d3.

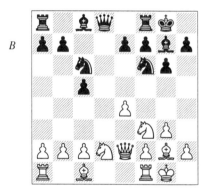

9...♗g4 10 h3

I felt this was the critical move as otherwise Black could play ...♕d7 or ...♕c8 preventing h3 and enabling him to play ...♗h3 at an appropriate point.

10...♘d4!

This move is very much to the point. Instead 10...♗e6 or 10...♗xf3 would have been inconsistent.

11 ♕c4?!

11 ♕d1, retracting his earlier ♕d1-e2, would have been more sensible.

11...♗e6

After 11...b5?! 12 ♕xc5! ♗xf3 13 ♗xf3 ♗h6 14 c3! ♘c2 15 ♘b3! White is well placed.

12 ♕d3

12 ♕xc5?? ♘d7 leaves White in big trouble.

12...♘d7 13 c3?! *(D)*

13 ♘xd4 is probably better although after 13...cxd4 14 f4 ♘c5 I would have felt more comfortable with my position.

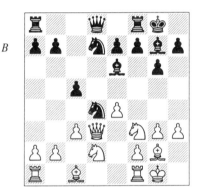

13...c4! 14 ♕b1

14 ♘xc4!? ♘c5 15 ♕e3 ♘xf3+ 16 ♗xf3 ♗xc4 17 ♕xc5 ♗xf1 18 ♔xf1 is not trivial but Black is obviously better.

14...♘e2+ 15 ♔h2 ♘c5

15...♕b6?! was very tempting but I was worried about 16 ♘g5!, when the position is not clear at all.

16 ♖e1 ♘xc1

16...♕d3 was also possible, but after 17 ♕xd3 cxd3 18 ♘g5, although White is very cramped and a little tied up, I couldn't see a clear way through his defences.

17 ♖xc1 ♘d3 18 ♖f1 ♕a5!

Stopping ♘g5 and lining up threats on the a1-h8 diagonal.

19 ♕c2 ♖fd8

Later on in the game I was a little worried (possibly unreasonably) about White playing ♘h4, f4 and f5 when I may have preferred my rook on f8 to defend on the kingside.

20 ♘h4 ♘xb2 21 ♘b1 ♘a4 22 ♖c1 ♖d3

22...♘c5 was quite possibly even stronger.

23 ♗f1

Now 23...♗xc3 would have left Black very much on top.

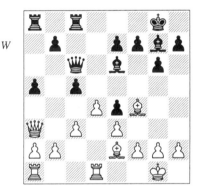

Baker – S. Buckley
Bristol Ch 1998

Black had just played 14...a7-a5, when a long, hard battle could be expected. In reply I played the harmless-looking...

15 dxc5

...and Black made the immediate and natural recapture.

15...♕xc5??

Black's position would still be tenable after 15...h6 and 16...♔h7 before capturing back.

16 ♖d8+!

White wins material.

Now let's look at two positions where a decision needs to be taken on how to proceed and a plan formed:

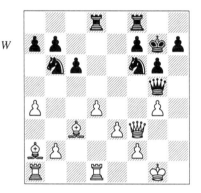

Baker – Summerscale
Hastings Challengers 1997/8

My first thought here was that Black was a lot better despite my bishop-pair. In particular, my dark-squared bishop seemed a poor piece, and on top of that my pawns on a4 and g4 were hanging and ...h5 might also be quite unpleasant to meet. There followed...

19 d5! ♘xa4!

19...♘xd5? 20 ♗xd5 ♖xd5 21 ♖xd5 cxd5 22 ♕f4! h6 23 ♕xg5 hxg5 24 f4! and White wins material.

20 ♗xf6+ ♕xf6 21 ♕xf6+ ♔xf6 22 dxc6 bxc6?!

Black should prefer 22...♖xd1+! 23 ♖xd1 bxc6 24 ♖d6+ ♔g5! 25 ♖xc6

♘xb2 26 ♖a6, reaching an equal position.

23 ♖xd8 ♖xd8 24 ♗xf7 ♔xf7

24...♘xb2!? 25 ♖xa7 leads to an ending that is difficult to judge, but White should be no worse.

25 ♖xa4 ♖d7 26 ♔g2

26 ♖a6 ♖c7 27 b4 ♔e6 28 b5 ♔d5 29 bxc6 ♔c5! and as ...♔b5 cannot be prevented, the position remains balanced.

½-½

Although there still remains a lot of play, I think both players had had enough.

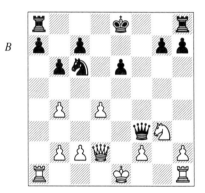

M. Houska – Baker
Cardiff 1998

It is clear that Black is nicely placed but the question is: what should he play next? 15...♖d8, 15...0-0, 15...0-0-0 and 15...e5 all seem viable and attractive. This is where a sharp eye, judgement and planning come into their own. As the game shows, Black's position is not only attractive but almost completely winning!

15...0-0-0! 16 c3 e5 17 b5 exd4! 18 bxc6 dxc3 19 ♕xc3 ♕g2!!

This 'quiet' move, not even involving a capture, is enough to seal White's fate. It was necessary to envisage this move prior to 15...0-0-0 or White would have had a perfectly satisfactory position. As it is, White is now busted. I used twenty minutes on this move, and felt this was time well invested. Note that it is best to use time to find the best lines from a position of strength. A lot of players seem to use their time only when they it is too late and their position is already beyond repair.

20 ♖f1 ♖he8+ 21 ♘e2 ♕e4 22 ♕h3+ ♔b8 23 ♕e3 ♕c2

Now the threats against d2 and e2 cannot be prevented.

24 ♖c1 ♕xb2

White could well have resigned at this point.

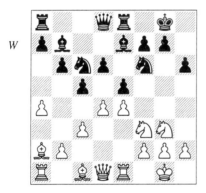

W

Baker – DeCoverly
Torquay 1998

Black has just played 13...♘a5-c6. Here I needed to decide on the best way to continue. In the end I found:

14 dxc5!

After 14 d5 White would have more space and better development. However, I have something else in mind.

14...dxc5

Not 14...bxc5? 15 ♕b3, when b7 and f7 are hanging.

15 ♕b3 ♖f8

Black is forced to retract his earlier move ...♖f8-e8, thus taking away the natural retreat for his dark-squared bishop. This denies him the plan of ...♗f8, ...g6, and ...♗g7.

16 ♘f5 ♕c7 17 ♗xh6!

The logical follow-up to White's previous play now that h6 is not indirectly defended by a bishop on f8.

17...♘a5

17...gxh6 18 ♘xh6+ ♔h7 19 ♘xf7 is not attractive for Black but may be better than the text-move.

18 ♕d1! gxh6 19 ♕d2! ♘h7

19...♗xe4 leads to a slightly prettier version of the same finish as the game after 20 ♖xe4! ♘xe4 21 ♕xh6 ♗f6 22 ♘g5! ♘xg5 23 ♕g6+.

20 ♕xh6 ♗f6 21 ♘g5! ♘xg5 22 ♕g6+ 1-0

The light-squared bishop, which had been lurking on the a2-g8 diagonal since the opening, finally proves its worth!

Next we will look at the conclusion of another of my own games. Although this is closer to an endgame than a middlegame, the 'finishing technique' is more relevant to middlegame play.

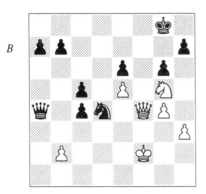

Varley – Baker
Newport 1999

Black needs to deal with the threat of ♕f7+ and ♕xh7#.

31...♕c2+!

Much clearer than 31...♕d7, besides which if things go wrong Black can always settle for the perpetual check! This is an important point as it is always nice to have some sort of 'safety net' if you cannot analyse a position to a conclusion.

32 ♔f1 ♕b1+ 33 ♔g2 ♕xb2+ 34 ♔f1 ♕b1+ 35 ♔g2 ♕g1+!

Forcibly swapping off the queens into a totally won knight and pawn ending.

0-1

In the following diagram, Black has just played 25...♗d4x♙b2 and hopes that with a pawn for the exchange, the bishop-pair and a superior pawn-structure, he may hold the balance despite the small material deficit. This type of position can 'slip' easily but is bread and butter for the master.

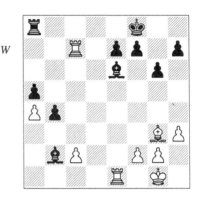

Summerscale – Van Vaalen
Hastings Challengers 1998/9

26 ♗e5!

White offers to exchange Black's powerful dark-squared bishop and thus dramatically improve the position of his rook from e1. If Black avoids the exchange, then the white bishop on e5 will be a dominant piece compared with its counterpart.

26...♗a3 27 ♗f4 ♖c8

Unfortunately, returning the bishop to its key diagonal by 27...♗b2 allows 28 ♗h6+ ♔e8 29 ♗g5, when Black is forced to exchange with 29...♗f6, making White's technical task far simpler.

28 ♖xe6!!

Knowing when to return material to make life as easy as possible takes excellent judgement and can save a lot of hard work. In this case the fact that Black's pawns are tied down to a5 and b4, i.e. dark squares (the same colour as White's bishop), is the deciding factor.

28...♖xc7 29 ♗xc7 fxe6 30 ♗xa5

White is now in effect just a passed pawn to the good as Black's kingside pawn-majority is for all intents and purposes immobile and worthless.

30...♔e8 31 ♔f1 ♔d7 32 ♔e2 ♔c6 33 ♔d3 ♔d5 34 ♗d8 e5 35 f3!

Stopping any further king penetration by Black. The greedy 35 ♗xe7 is winning as well but can wait a move.

35...♗b2 36 ♗xe7 ♗c3 37 a5 1-0

Black cannot afford further concessions.

Our next instructive example comes from Grandmaster Mark Hebden. In a position with opposite-side castling, he probes on several fronts, looking for every opportunity to punish his opponent for any lapse.

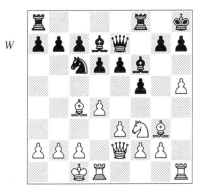

Hebden – T. Wall
Hastings Challengers 1998/9

After a fairly unusual variation of the Dutch we have reached a position in which Black appears solid and White's kingside attacking chances seem a long way off.

14 ♘h4 ♗xh4!

This move 'feels' right in as much as it removes White's dangerous knight, and conceding the bishop-pair is not an unreasonable strategy in a fairly closed position, such as we seem to have here.

15 ♗xh4 ♕f7 16 h6!

This thrust forces Black to weaken his dark squares, especially along the a1-h8 diagonal, as this is, from Black's viewpoint, a lesser evil than opening up his kingside.

16...g6 17 ♕d2 ♘e7 18 ♕c3 d5?!

Black keeps the position closed but creates a permanent weakness on d5, a backward pawn on e6 and makes his light-squared bishop a relatively poor piece.

19 ♗e2 ♖fc8 20 ♗g5 a5 21 ♔b1 b6 22 f3!

Keeping the e4 and g4 options available.

22...♘g8 23 e4 ♘f6 24 exf5 exf5 25 ♖he1 c6 26 ♗d3 ♖e8 27 ♖e5! *(D)*

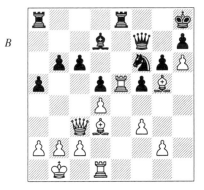

White doubles rooks on the e-file, exploiting the fact that Black doesn't want to exchange on e5 and open the a1-h8 diagonal.

27...♖e6 28 ♖xe6!

Now Black cannot recapture with his other rook, and so White is able to keep a firm grip on the e-file.

28...♕xe6 29 ♖e1 ♕f7 30 ♖e5 ♖e8 31 a4!

White is content to adopt a 'sit and wait' policy for the time being. This move is useful as it ties down Black's queenside ready for the prospective ending, and also stops any queenside thrust by Black during the major-piece middlegame.

31...♔g8 32 ♕e1

Now White seizes complete control of the e-file.

32...♘h5 33 g4!

Thematically prising open Black's kingside.

33...fxg4 34 fxg4 ♖xe5 35 ♕xe5 ♗xg4 36 ♕b8+ ♕f8 37 ♕xb6

By a series of consistent moves, White exchanges into an ending where Black's queenside pawns are ripe for the picking.

37...♗d7 38 ♕xa5 1-0

Black resigned rather than suffer any further, waiting for White's a-pawn to hit the eighth rank.

Remain razor-sharp and use your time wisely in a position where you feel you are well placed but face a decision or a choice. This often pays dividends. Try also to find the continuation that is consistent with your previous play – more often than not, 'little tactics', moves or lines for your opponent that you hadn't previously

considered, will still work out in your favour.

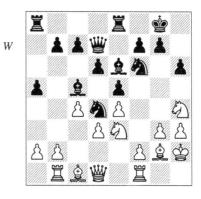

Friedgood – Pritchett
British League (4NCL) 1998/9

Black has just played 14...♘c6-d4. The opening has now finished and White must form a plan. An attempt at queenside expansion is possible but hardly practical, so White correctly goes for extra space on the kingside ready for the attack.

15 f4! ♕d8

More appealing than 15...exf4, when White not only gets a dangerous central pawn-majority but the g-file to use for attacking purposes as well.

16 f5

White consistently opens up the c1-h6 diagonal and prepares a g4-g5 advance.

16...♗d7 17 ♘g4

Pushing another piece towards the black king.

17...c6

Naturally, Black rejects the idea of continuing 17...♘xg4+, which would open up the h-file for White to use at his leisure.

18 ♘xf6+ ♕xf6 19 ♕h5

Another piece heading in the right direction.

19...♗b6 20 g4 ♗d8 *(D)*

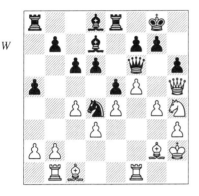

W

21 g5!

White delays no further and prises open Black's kingside.

21...hxg5 22 ♘g6!

A natural type of move for the King's Indian player!

22...fxg6

Or ♕h8# was coming.

23 fxg6 ♘f5 24 ♗xg5!

The crowning glory of White's previous play.

24...♕xg5 25 ♕h7+ ♔f8 26 ♖xf5+!

Removing the defender of g7.

26...♗xf5?

26...♕f6 is the best way of shoring up Black's kingside although I still wouldn't fancy his long-term chances.

27 ♕h8+ ♔e7 28 ♕xg7+ 1-0

28...♔e6 29 ♕f7# follows.

This was a powerfully played attack with some nice tactical points but

the 'unsung' heroes, 15 f4 and 16 f5, should not go without their just recognition.

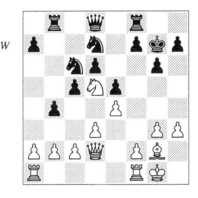

W

M.Turner – Sowray
British League (4NCL) 1998/9

Black had just committed himself with 15...e7-e5?!. We have now arrived at a middlegame position reminiscent of a Closed Sicilian (rather than the Modern Defence, which was actually the one played in the game). Normally White will try for play on the kingside. Black will try to neutralize this, while aiming for counterplay by queenside expansion.

16 f4 f6

16...f5 17 fxe5 dxe5!? (17...♘dxe5 18 exf5 would leave Black with serious kingside weaknesses, a hole on e6 and an isolated f-pawn) 18 exf5 gxf5 leads to a position which is difficult to judge as Black's hanging pawns on e5 and f5 may well be a source of weakness as much as strength.

17 h4

Probing.

17...♘b6

Removing White's knight from d5 but at the cost of taking his own knight away from the centre and kingside.

18 ♘e3!

Black achieves his aim, but at the cost of misplacing his own knight. It turns out that the white knight can do good work from e3, retaining options of operating on the kingside or hopping back into d5 should the need or desire arise.

18...♖b7!

Usefully preparing to swing over to the kingside and double on the f-file if required.

19 ♖ae1

Saving the f5 advance for later, although the immediate thrust must have been very tempting.

19...♘d4 20 ♖f2

Again 20 f5 was an option, as was 20 c3 with the intention of immediately kicking away the black knight. Possibly White wanted to continue building up, retaining both options until one became clearly better than the other or an even more appealing alternative reared its head.

20...♖bf7 21 h5! *(D)*

Finally committing himself to a plan.

21...♕d7

Obviously avoiding 21...gxh5, when after 22 c3 White's knight will aggressively penetrate on f5.

22 ♔h2 a5

Black expands on the queenside, hoping White will be unable to make further progress on the kingside.

23 ♖ef1 ♕e8 24 ♗h3!

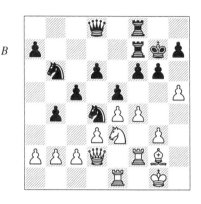

B

A thematic improvement of the light-squared bishop. White both takes control of the h3-c8 diagonal and has ideas of eventually doing damage on the light squares surrounding Black's king.

24...♕b5 25 c3

Eventually the 'kicking away' manoeuvre pays dividends as White's bishop penetrates via e6.

25...♘c6 *(D)*

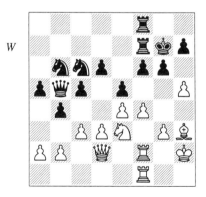

W

26 ♗e6! ♖e7 27 ♗d5

This manoeuvre has the eventual aim of re-occupying d5 with a knight which will take a while for Black to remove.

27...♘xd5 28 ♘xd5 ♖ef7 29 ♔g2 bxc3 30 bxc3 exf4?!

Eventually Black cracks and concedes the e6-square although by now Black's position was looking shaky.

31 ♘xf4 ♖b8?

31...♖e8 was necessary.

32 hxg6 hxg6 33 ♘e6+ ♔g8 34 ♕h6 1-0

The end has come swiftly, with Black's king position falling apart. A well-played game by Matthew Turner, who knows exactly how to handle these type of positions.

The next example sees Tony Miles going into a position that looks fraught with danger only to unleash a powerful counter-idea.

Miles – Sorin
Matanzas Capablanca mem 1995

1 e4 e5 2 ♘f3 ♘c6 3 d4 exd4 4 ♘xd4 ♘f6 5 ♘c3 ♗c5 6 ♘xc6 bxc6 7 ♗d3 d6 8 0-0 ♘g4

8...♘d7 9 ♗e2 0-0 10 ♘a4 ♗b6 11 b3 ♕h4 12 ♘xb6 axb6 13 f3 ♗a6 14 c4 c5 15 ♗b2 slightly favoured White in Miles-Hebden, London Lloyds Bank 1994. This time Miles's opponent adopts a more aggressive set-up.

9 ♗f4 g5

9...♕f6!? is also possible.

10 ♗d2 ♕f6 11 ♕e2 ♕e5

11...♕h6!? 12 h3 ♘e5 seems an alternative way to occupy the e5-square.

12 g3 ♕e6 *(D)*

With the idea of 13...♘xh2!.

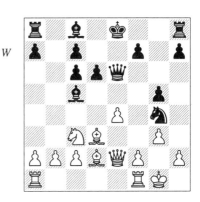

13 ♘a4! ♗d4 14 c3 ♕h6 15 h4 ♗f6 16 e5!

A typical motif: White opens up the position in response to a flank attack since he is better developed.

16...♘xe5 17 hxg5 ♗xg5 18 f4 ♕h3 19 ♗e4! ♕xg3+ 20 ♕g2 ♕xg2+ 21 ♗xg2

From this point on the win is easy.

21...♗h6 22 fxe5 ♗xd2 23 ♗xc6+ ♗d7 24 ♗xa8 ♗xa4 25 exd6 cxd6 26 ♖f2 ♗g5 27 ♖e1+ ♔f8 28 ♗d5 ♗e8 29 ♖f5 f6 30 ♖f3 h5 31 c4 h4 32 ♖b3 ♗f4 33 ♖xe8+ 1-0

In our next example (*see diagram on following page*) we see the depth of opening preparation in top-level chess:

This position arose from a topical variation of the Sicilian Pelikan. Black needs to maintain activity on the kingside as, despite his outpost on e5, his position is precarious and full of latent weaknesses.

21 ♖xf3!

Not the most obvious recapture. In Anand-Kramnik, Linares 1998 White

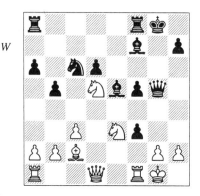

Topalov – Van Wely
Wijk aan Zee 1999

had played 21 ♕xf3 and the game was drawn after 28 moves. It was thought that Anand could have improved at move 26 of that game, but perhaps the improvement was to be found even earlier with the text-move.

21...♗h5 22 ♘c7!

Now it looks as though White will win the exchange back on c7 or by playing a timely ♘e6, forking f8 and g5. However, Black can 'save' the exchange but at a cost. For Black to survive the middlegame he needs to hang on to the extra material, as otherwise his position is riddled with weaknesses without the extra material to compensate.

22...♗f4 23 ♕d5+ ♔h8 24 ♖xf4! ♕xf4 25 ♖e1

Now Black has to do something about his loose c6-knight, f5-pawn and a8-rook.

25...♖ac8 26 ♘e6

After 26 ♕xc6?! ♕e5, in spite of White's extra material, it is difficult

for him to unravel, e.g. 27 ♕d7 ♖fd8, when White must retreat his queen back to c7.

26...♕h4

Saving the exchange due to the threat of ...♕xe1+.

27 g3 ♖g8 28 ♘xf5

White has knight and pawn for rook together with threats against d6 and attacking chances. As the game shows, this is more than adequate.

28...♕c4 29 ♕xd6 ♖g6 30 ♘e7!

This subtle tactic decides the game in White's favour

30...♘xe7 31 ♕e5+ ♔g8 32 ♗xg6 1-0

The threat of mate on g7 causes Black's position to fall apart.

Finally a game which illustrates a thematic sacrifice that shows White the error of his ways:

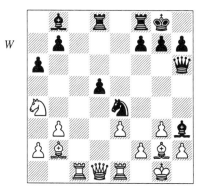

Poluliakhov – Belozerov
Moscow Geller mem 1999

This position came from a Symmetrical Tarrasch.

23 ♘c5??

In principle it is correct for White to try to improve his knight and to put pressure on Black's queenside in the hope that Black will feel obliged to exchange off his powerfully placed knight on e4. However, as often is the case in these types of position, White must keep complete control of the tactics before he can hope to make anything of his positional advantages (i.e. Black's isolated d-pawn and White's superior dark-squared bishop).

23...♗xg2 24 ♔xg2 ♘xf2! *(D)*

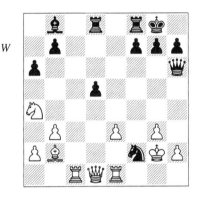

All of a sudden White's king looks very exposed.

25 ♔xf2 ♕xh2+ 26 ♔f3

26 ♔f1 ♕h3+ 27 ♔g1 (27 ♔e2 would transpose to the game, with the insignificant difference that White retains his g-pawn) 27...♕xg3+ 28 ♔f1 ♕h3+ 29 ♔f2 (29 ♔g1 ♗h2+ 30 ♔h1 ♗g3+ 31 ♔g1 ♕h2+ 32 ♔f1 ♕f2#) 29...♗g3+ 30 ♔e2 ♕g2+ 31 ♔d3 ♗xe1 and White's position falls apart.

26...♕xg3+ 27 ♔e2 ♕g2+ 28 ♔d3 ♕xb2

Three pawns down and with an inferior position, there is little for White to play for.

29 ♘xb7 ♖c8 0-1

It is clear that 23 ♘c5 was disastrous in view of Black's tactical response. However, many of us would as Black have been guilty of 'missing the moment' and would have slid slowly backwards instead, claiming afterwards that the whole opening line was 'positionally inferior' and that we hadn't a chance. As many examples in this chapter show, we must seize our chances with both hands.

Middlegame Exercises

It is now time for you to tackle a few exercises. While all these positions involve tactics, you also need to judge the positions correctly to determine how best to proceed. Each position needs careful analysis to back up the move you would like to play with concrete variations. After all you cannot take back a move once you have played it, even if you want to change your mind! Once you have decided on the move you would play, turn to pages 131-4 to see how the game actually continued and to compare your analysis with the notes given there.

1
W

How is it best for White to proceed?

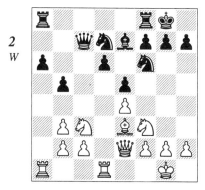

2
W

How should White continue the battle for control of the d5-square?

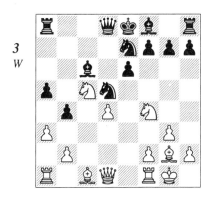

3
W

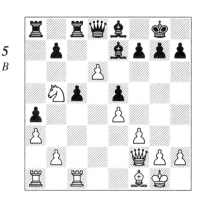

5
B

White (to play) has a tempting sacrificial idea that is reminiscent of Sicilian positions. However, make sure you have worked out the necessary follow-up.

Black (to move) needs to decide how best to deal with the white pawn on d6.

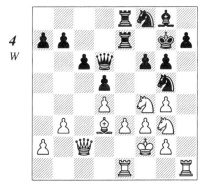

4
W

6
W

Black has carelessly just moved his queen to a spot suitable for a future knight fork. How should White exploit this tactical theme? (Two solutions)

White is to move. His position looks quite inviting as Black is more than a little tied up, but how should he best proceed?

3 Endgame Technique

'...and the rest was just a matter of technique' is a phrase that I've heard people use on many occasions, normally before they failed to convert their advantage or at least only did so with a little help from their opponents.

Mating with Bishop and Knight

In this section I am going to start by looking at ♔+♗+♘ vs ♔. In case you think this is too trivial, I can recall one very strong player who needed to beat International Master Colin Crouch in this ending for an IM norm and failed. Recently in a British League game, Grandmaster Aaron Summerscale managed by excellent technique to hold on to his final pawn and thus avoided having to win this ending. Afterwards he said "I've taught it enough at school, so I know how to do it, but I still wanted to avoid it!"

First of all, the diagrams in the next column show you the two basic positions that you should aim for.

The vital point to note is that it is only possible to force mate in, or adjacent to, a corner square that is of the same colour as the bishop. We refer to the two light-squared corners as the 'right' corners, and the two dark-squared corners as the 'wrong' corners.

If you have a dark-squared bishop, then the descriptions are of course reversed.

There are two other types of mating positions but they cannot be forced during the normal course of events.

Let's start by looking at a position which could be regarded at fairly unfavourable for the aggressor:

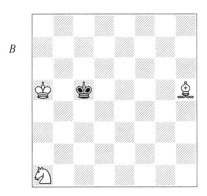

We will look at the technique required in two stages:

Stage 1: Force the opponent to the side and corner. We shall assume the opponent walks, when forced, to the 'wrong' corner (i.e. a dark-squared corner).

Stage 2: Force him into the 'right' corner, where we can finish him off.

During both of these stages we will combine the pieces, in particular the bishop and knight, to form a barrier which the enemy king cannot get past.

Stage 1

1...♔c6

1...♔c4 2 ♗f7+ is similar.

2 ♘b3 ♔d6

2...♔d5 3 ♔b5 ♔d6 4 ♔c4 ♔e5 5 ♘c5 ♔f5 6 ♔d5 ♔g5 7 ♗f3 ♔f5 8 ♘e6 (notice the 'barrier' on d4-e4-f4-g4-g5-h5) 8...♔f6 9 ♗e4 (and now on e5-f5-g5-g6-g7) 9...♔e7 10 ♔e5 ♔f7 11 ♘f4 ♔g7 12 ♗d5 ♔h7 13 ♔f6 ♔h8 14 ♘g6+ ♔h7 15 ♗e6 and, now that the king is on the edge of the board, play moves on to Stage 2.

3 ♔b5 ♔d5 4 ♗f7+ ♔e5

4...♔d6 5 ♗c4 ♔e5 6 ♔c5 ♔e4 7 ♔d6 (barrier on e2-d2-d3-d4-d5-e5) 7...♔f5 8 ♗d3+ ♔f6 9 ♘d2 ♔f7 10 ♘c4 ♔f6 11 ♘e5 ♔g7 12 ♔e7 ♔h8 13 ♔f6 ♔g8 14 ♘f7 and again play proceeds to Stage 2.

5 ♔c5 ♔f6 6 ♗c4 ♔e5 7 ♘d2 ♔f4 8 ♔d6 *(D)*

8...♔f5

8...♔e3 9 ♘b3 (barrier!) 9...♔f4 10 ♗d3 ♔g5 11 ♔e5 ♔h6 12 ♔f6 ♔h5 13 ♗f5 ♔h4 14 ♔g6 ♔g3 15 ♔g5 ♔f3 16 ♗c2 (barrier – this time on d1-d2-d3-d4-e4) 16...♔e3 17 ♔g4 ♔e2 18 ♔f4 ♔f2 19 ♗d1! (this is another recurrent theme – one of transferring the bishop's control of a square {this time d1} from one diagonal, a4-d1, to another – h5-d1) 19...♔e1 20 ♗f3 ♔f2 21 ♘d4 will lead to positions similar to those towards the end of Stage 2, when the enemy king is already well on its way to the 'right' corner.

9 ♗d3+ ♔f6 10 ♘f3

Barrier.

10...♔f7 11 ♔e5 ♔g7

11...♔e7 12 ♗c4 would once again lead to positions covered in Stage 2.

12 ♘g5 ♔g8 13 ♔f6 ♔f8 14 ♘f7 ♔g8 *(D)*

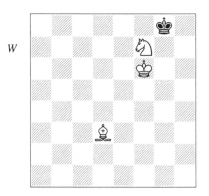

Stage 2

15 ♗f5 ♔f8 16 ♗h7!

It is necessary to stop Black being able to return to the g8-square but it is equally vital to use the bishop to do so, as it is the long-range piece. Instead 16 ♘h6? would leave the knight on the edge of the board and stranded out of play.

16...♔e8 17 ♘e5 ♔d8

17...♔f8 18 ♘d7+ ♔e8 19 ♔e6 ♔d8 20 ♔d6 ♔e8 21 ♗g6+ (barrier!) 21...♔d8 22 ♘c5 ♔c8 23 ♗d3! (notice this repositioning of the bishop as in the note to Black's 8th move) 23...♔d8 24 ♗b5 ♔c8 25 ♗d7+ ♔b8 26 ♔c6 ♔a7 27 ♔c7 ♔a8 28 ♔b6 ♔b8 29 ♘a6+ ♔a8 30 ♗c6#.

18 ♔e6 ♔c7 19 ♘d7 ♔b7

19...♔c6 20 ♗d3! (barrier) 20...♔b7 21 ♔d6 ♔c8 22 ♘c5 ♔b8 23 ♔d7 ♔a7 24 ♔c7 ♔a8 25 ♔b6 ♔b8 26 ♗a6 ♔a8 27 ♗b7+ ♔b8 28 ♘d7#.

20 ♗d3!

Barrier.

20...♔c6 21 ♗a6 ♔c7 22 ♗b5 ♔d8 23 ♘b6 ♔c7 24 ♘d5+

Barrier.

24...♔d8 25 ♔d6 ♔c8 26 ♔e7 ♔b7 27 ♔d7 ♔b8 28 ♗a6 ♔a7 29 ♗c8 ♔b8 30 ♘e7 ♔a7

30...♔a8 31 ♔c7 ♔a7 32 ♘c6+ ♔a8 33 ♗b7#.

31 ♔c7 ♔a8 32 ♗b7+

Not 32 ♘c6?? stalemate!

32...♔a7 33 ♘c6#

Rook and Pawn vs Rook

The other topic that I want to cover in this section is rook and pawn endings, in particular ♖+♙ vs ♖. The main reason for this is that they are so common and, despite there being only five pieces left on the board, can be a source of total confusion. There are good, complete reference books on this subject, notably *Secrets of Rook Endings* by John Nunn, and so I cannot expect to cover this ending in detail here. However, a good general understanding of some of the basic principles will hold you in good stead. After these I will whet your appetite with one or two 'meatier' examples. The general rule is that if the defending king controls the queening square it should be drawn and if the attacking king controls the queening square it should be won (one notable exception is the rook's pawn, which has considerations of its own).

Let us look first of all at one of the standard drawing techniques:

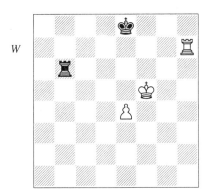

Now the basic technique for Black is to keep the rook on the third rank until the pawn reaches e6 at which point the rook goes to its eighth rank, ready to start checking the white king from behind, since at this point, with the pawn on e6, the white king has nowhere to hide. One of the important factors for Black to keep in mind is when it would be safe to exchange off into a drawn king and pawn ending – generally this means one in which he holds the opposition.

1 e5 ♖a6 2 e6 ♖a1

Not 2...♖b6?? 3 ♔f6 ♔d8 4 ♖h8+ ♔c7 5 ♔f7 and White wins.

3 ♔f6 ♖f1+ 4 ♔e5 ♖e1+ 5 ♔d6 ♖d1+

White cannot make progress. Note that even if White could interpose his rook, Black could exchange them off and draw the king and pawn ending.

The next example shows one of the exceptions to the general rule, in that the defender's rook must stay passively placed in order to stop the back-rank threats:

1...♖c8

1...♔g8 2 ♖g2+ ♔f8 3 e7+ ♔e8 4 ♖g8+ ♔d7 5 ♖xb8, etc.

2 ♖h2 ♔g8 3 ♖g2+ ♔h8

3...♔f8 4 e7+ ♔e8 5 ♖g8+ ♔d6 6 ♖xc8 and White wins.

4 ♔f7 ♖c7+ 5 e7

Black will be forced to give up his rook for White's pawn.

The most important position of all in terms of winning technique is known as the **Lucena Position**, and is as follows:

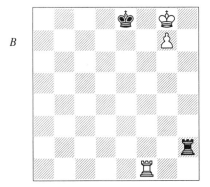

1...♖h3

1...♖e2 2 ♖h1 followed by ♔h8 and g8♕ wins.

2 ♖f4!

A plan aptly known as 'building the bridge'.

2...♖h1 3 ♖e4+ ♔d7 4 ♔f7 ♖f1+ 5 ♔g6 ♖g1+ 6 ♔f6 ♖f1+

Alternatively: 6...♖g2 7 ♖e5 with the idea of ♖g5, or 6...♔d6 7 ♖d4+ ♔c6 8 ♖d8 ♖f1+ 9 ♔e5 ♖e1+ 10 ♔f4, etc.

7 ♔g5 ♖g1+ 8 ♖g4

White wins.

Now it is time to look at some less obviously clear-cut positions:

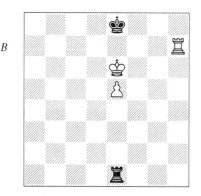

1...♔f8!

Black correctly chooses to go to the 'short side', the principle being to leave the long side available for his rook to give checks. 1...♔d8 doesn't actually lose in this position but is a step in the wrong direction and requires more accurate defence. Compare this with the next example.

2 ♖h8+

2 ♔d6 doesn't achieve anything as 3 e6 would allow 3...♖d1+, etc.

2...♔g7 3 ♖e8

The best try is to 'free' the white king from its duty to guard the e-pawn. 3 ♖a8 ♖e2 4 ♔d6 ♔f7! 5 ♖a7+ ♔e8 6 ♔e6, etc., gets nowhere.

3...♖a1!

Now 4 ♔d7 allows 4...♖a7+, when White can make no further progress.

4 ♖d8 ♖e1!

Black draws.

Let us now look at an example where the defending side is losing due to his rook having to go to the 'short side'.

1 ♔f7! ♖h1

Otherwise White can play e6 and ♔e7.

2 ♖g8

Not 2 e6? ♖h7+ 3 ♔g6 ♖h1 drawing.

2...♖h7+ 3 ♖g7 ♖h8

One of the important differences: Black loses if he exchanges rooks and enters the king and pawn ending.

4 &e7!

Not 4 e6? &d6! 5 e7 &d7 6 &g1
&h7+ 7 &f8, when 7...&h8+ draws,
but not 7...&xe7?? 8 &d1+ &e6 9 &e1+
and White wins.

4...&c6

What else?

5 e6 &c7 6 &f7

Zugzwang!

**6...&g8 7 &f1 &g7+ 8 &f6 &g2 9
&d1**

White wins since the black king is
cut off.

White has the threat of &g1+ but
Black is able to draw precisely because his rook is on the a-file.

1...&a7+ 2 &d7

2 &e8 &f6 and 2 &d6 &f8 both
draw.

2...&a1 3 &e8+

After 3 &d6+ &f6 4 &f7+ &g6 5
&c7 (5 &f2 &a6+) 5...&f6 White is
not making progress, since 6 e7 may
be answered by 6...&d1+ 7 &c6 &f7
halting the pawn.

Alternatively, 3 &d6 is answered by
3...&a8! (3...&a2? 4 &e8! would win

as after 4...&f6, the advance 5 e7+ is
check).

**3...&f6 4 e7 &e6! 5 &f8 &f1+! 6
&e8 &a1**

Black draws.

Next an example of how White can
win if **he** controls the a-file:

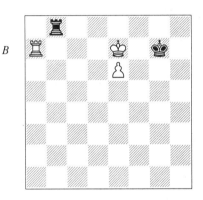

This is an extremely interesting position. First of all, if it is Black to move
he is in zugzwang:

1...&g6

White wins after 1...&g8 2 &a1 or
1...&b1 2 &a8! &b7+ 3 &d6 &b6+ 4
&d7 &b7+ 5 &c6 &e7 6 &d6.

**2 &a1! &b7+ 3 &d6 &b6+ 4 &d7
&b7+ 5 &c6 &b2**

Or 5...&b8 6 &c7 &e8 7 &d7 and
White wins. Alternatively 5...&e7 6
&d6 wins as 6...&f6 is of course met
by 7 &f1+.

6 &e1!

Now the passed pawn is dominant
as the black king cannot return to help
stop it queening.

6...&b8 7 &d7! &b7+ 8 &c8 &e7

8...&a7 9 e7 &a8+ 10 &d7, etc.

9 ♔d8 ♔f6 10 ♖f1+! ♔xe6 11 ♖e1+

White has finally achieved his aim.

However, if it is White to move in the original position, the win requires a little more cunning:

1 ♔d6+! ♔f6

1...♔g6 2 ♖a1! transposes back to the first variation while 1...♔f8 loses to 2 ♔d7 ♖e8 3 ♖a1, etc.

2 ♔d7! ♔g7 3 ♔e7!

White, by means of a subtle triangulation, has transposed back to the original position with Black to move now! As previous analysis showed, he cannot save the position. The conclusion therefore is that control of the a-file (or h-file if originally White had a d-pawn) is of absolute importance.

The next position was originally analysed as a study by Kopaev, and later arose over the board in Rohde-Cramling, Innsbruck jr Wch 1977.

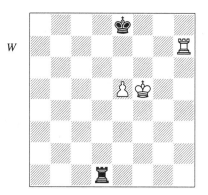

Kopaev
1955

In the subsequent analysis, some lines are left without an assessment. This is because they have already been reached in the previous examples, and I leave it as an exercise for the reader to find them.

1 ♔e6!

1 ♔f6? ♖e1 is only a draw.

1...♔f8

1...♔d8 2 ♖h8+ ♔c7 3 ♔e7 and White wins.

2 ♖f7+!

2 ♖a7? ♖e1 draws.

2...♔g8

2...♔e8 3 ♖a7 ♔f8 (3...♔d8 4 ♖a8+ ♔c7 5 ♔e7 is winning because now the black rook has to operate on the short side) 4 ♖a8+ ♔g7 5 ♔e7 ♖b1 6 e6.

3 ♖d7! ♖e1 4 ♔f6! ♖f1+ 5 ♔e7 ♖a1!

5...♖f7+ 6 ♔d6 ♖f8 (6...♖f1 7 e6 ♖d1+ 8 ♔e7 ♖a1 9 ♖d2) 7 e6 ♖a8 8 ♔e5! (8 ♔e7? ♔g7 draws) 8...♔f8 9 ♔f6 ♖b8 10 ♖f7+ ♔e8 11 ♖g7 ♔f8 12 e7+, etc.

6 ♖d2! ♖a7+ 7 ♔f6 ♖f7+ 8 ♔e6 ♖f1

Black would like to capture the a-file, but 8...♖a7 fails to 9 ♖d8+ ♔g7 10 ♖d7+.

9 ♖a2! ♔g7

9...♖e1 10 ♔f6 (for the third time White's king goes to f6!) 10...♖f1+ 11 ♔e7 ♖f7+ 12 ♔d6, etc.

10 ♖a7+ ♔g6 11 ♖a8 ♔g7 12 ♔e7 ♖f7+

Or 12...♖b1 13 e6.

13 ♔d6

White has finally reached a clearly winning position.

Practical Endgames

Before we leave this chapter, let's look at a few examples of endgames from actual play.

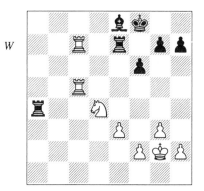

Baker – Devereaux
Newport 1999

Black has just played 35...♖e4-e7 and White must choose how best to proceed. The king and pawn ending would be easily won but right now White must decide whether to aim for the rook and pawn ending or the minor-piece ending. Generally the minor-piece ending should offer better chances, but here White has a subtle manoeuvre which forces Black's rook into total passivity.

36 ♖xe7 ♔xe7 37 ♖c7+ ♗d7 38 ♘b3!

Threatening 39 ♖xd7+ ♔xd7 40 ♘c5+, winning the rook. Moreover, if Black plays his rook anywhere but g4 then ♘c5 ♔d6, ♖xd7+ ♔xc5, ♖xg7 leads to an easily won ♖+4♙ vs ♖+2♙ ending.

38...♖g4 39 h3!

Forcing the black rook to a worse square.

39...♖g6 40 ♘c5 ♔d6 41 ♖xd7+ ♔xc5 42 f4!

Even further reducing the squares available to the rook.

42...♔c6 43 ♖a7 h5 44 ♔f3 ♔b6 45 ♖f7 ♔c6 46 e4

The manoeuvre 46 ♖f8 ♖h6 47 ♖g8 g6 (47...♖h7 48 ♔e4 with the idea of ♔f5-g6) 48 ♔e4 ♔d6 49 f5 g5 50 ♖g6 winning, was very tempting.

46...♔c5 47 f5 ♖g5 48 ♔f4 1-0

Black cannot prevent e4-e5, etc.

Our next example is from a ♕+♙ ending. These can be particularly interesting and difficult. After the game it was thought that White was probably winning all the way along. However, a 'cunning defence' was then found, illustrating once more the importance of never giving up.

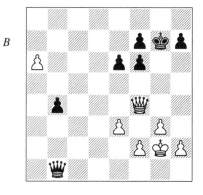

J. Cobb – Devereaux
Newport 1999

31...♕a2?

This seems very tempting as it clears the way for the b-pawn to queen while keeping an eye on White's a-pawn, which is further advanced. However, White has a clever idea in mind.

32 ♕g4+! ♔h6

Forced as after 32...♔f8 the b-pawn falls with check, and 32...♔h8 allows 33 ♕xb4 with the threat of ♕f8#.

33 ♕xb4 ♕xa6 34 ♕f8+ ♔g6 35 ♕g8+

Winning the f7-pawn.

35...♔h6 36 ♕xf7

White is well in control as Black, although only a pawn down, has no counterplay, i.e., a passed pawn or concrete threats of perpetual check. I will show you the remaining moves to illustrate the point.

36...♕c6+ 37 ♔g1 e5

As White was very short of time, Black was trying to avoid giving him easy moves. However, 37...♕c1+ 38 ♔g2 ♕c6+ 39 ♔h3 ♕f3 40 ♕xe6 ♕xf2 41 ♕e4 ♔g7 42 ♕f4 may have been a better try for Black – although White has good chances, Black's weaknesses are not as pronounced as in the game.

38 h4 ♕f3 39 ♕g8 e4?!

This move just creates a further liability.

40 ♕b8

With the idea of ♕f4+ exchanging queens. This is a recurring motif as swapping off to a won ♔+♙ ending is one of the easiest ways for White to realize his advantage.

40...♔g7 41 ♕f4 ♕d1+ 42 ♔g2 ♕d5 43 g4 ♕c4 44 ♕f5 ♕c6 45 h5

♔h6 46 ♔g3 ♔g7 47 ♔f4 ♕c2 48 h6+! ♔f7

48...♔xh6 allows 49 ♕xf6#.

49 ♕xh7+ ♔f8 50 ♔g3! ♕b1 51 ♔g2! 1-0

Having gone forward and done its job, the white king returns to its safe haven.

But if we go back to the original position Black has...

31...b3 32 ♕g4+!

After 32 a7 ♕a1 it's difficult to see how White can make progress.

32...♕g6

32...♔h6 33 a7! (33 ♕f3 ♔g7 34 a7 b2 35 a8♕ ♕g6! draws since Black will queen and, if White tries to give mate by 36 ♕f4 b1♕ 37 ♕d6, then 37...♕be4+ exchanges off a pair of queens) 33...♕a1 34 ♕f3! ♕xa7 35 ♕xf6+ ♔h5 36 f3 mating.

33 ♕b4 ♕d3 34 a7 ♕a6 35 ♕g4+ ♔f8 36 ♕d4 ♔g7

White has problems realizing whatever advantage he may have.

Finally we will look at the conclusion of a fascinating encounter between International Masters Colin Crouch and Luke McShane (*see diagram on following page*).

Black's position looks precarious as White's h-pawn, combined with his more active rook and bishop-pair, looks menacing.

38 ♗xc6! ♖xg3!?

38...♗xc6 39 ♗xe5 offers Black little chance of activity or survival.

39 ♖h7+ ♔d6 40 ♗xd7 e4 41 ♗c8 ♖g1+ 42 ♔c2 ♖g2+ 43 ♔d1 e3

Crouch – McShane
British League (4NCL) 1998/9

Black must rely on his connected passed pawns to offer chances before White can coordinate and his material advantage decides the issue. I must admit that when I saw the position at this point, I assumed that White should be winning.

44 ♖d7+ ♔e5 45 ♗xb7 ♖d2+ 46 ♔e1 d3 47 ♗f3

47 ♖e7+!? ♔f4 (47...♔d4? 48 ♖e4+ ♔c3 49 ♖xe3 and, with White's bishop retreating to f3 if necessary, Black has lost any chance of counterplay) 48 ♖e4+ ♔f3 49 ♖d4+ ♔g3 50 ♗e4 ♖e2+ 51 ♔d1 ♖d2+ 52 ♔c1 ♖c2+ 53 ♔b1 e2! 54 ♖xd3+ ♔xh4 55 ♖e3 ♖d2 56 c5 ♖d1+ 57 ♔c2 e1♕ 58 ♖xe1 ♖xe1 59 ♔d3 may be good enough but is still not conclusive.

47...♖f2 48 ♗h5

48 ♖xd3?! ♖xf3 49 ♖d7 ♖h3 50 ♖xa7 ♔e4 51 ♖e7+ ♔d3 52 ♖d7+ ♔e4 53 a4 ♖xh4 54 b4 ♖h1+ 55 ♔e2 ♖h2+ 56 ♔d1 ♖h1+ 57 ♔c2?! (White may well do best to take the draw with

57 ♔e2) 57...e2 58 ♖e7+ ♔f3 leads to an inferior version of the game for White.

48...d2+ 49 ♔d1 ♖f1+ 50 ♔c2 ♖c1+ 51 ♔b2 ♔f4 52 ♖f7+ ♔g3 53 ♖xa7 d1♕ 54 ♗xd1 ♖xd1 55 ♖e7 ♔f3 56 ♔c3?! *(D)*

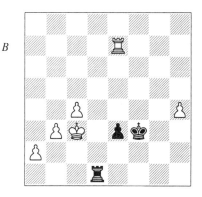

This may well be wrong. We are about to get a position where White has several pawns vs a lone rook, and I am not convinced that White should be trying to support his passed pawns with his king, rather than pushing the pawns straight away, hoping that the rook cannot cope with the pawn-mass on its own.

56...e2 57 a4 e1♕+

Black promotes for the second time in four moves!

58 ♖xe1 ♖xe1 *(D)*

59 c5

59 a5, pushing the outside passed pawn, or 59 ♔d4, abandoning the b-pawn but attempting to cut off the black king, looks more natural to me.

59...♔e4 60 ♔c4 ♔e5 61 ♔b5 ♖b1?

61...♔d5! 62 a5 ♖e8 seems to leave White awkwardly placed.

62 b4 ♔e6 63 h5

After 63 a5? ♔d7 64 a6 ♔c7 65 c6 ♖f1 White runs out of moves. Instead White aims for a position in which he hopes Black is unable to make progress.

63...♔d7 64 ♔c4 ♖h1 65 b5 ♖h4+!

This is a good move, forcing the white king to retreat, hence cutting it off from the pawns.

66 ♔b3 ♖xh5 67 c6+ ♔d6 68 ♔b4 ♖h4+ 69 ♔b3 ♔c5 70 ♔a3 *(D)*

The conclusion of the position is still not as trivial as it looks, due to the advanced position of White's b- and c-pawns.

70...♔b6 71 ♔b3 ♔c5 72 ♔a3 ♖h3+ 73 ♔b2 ♔b6 74 ♔a2 ♔a5 75 ♔b2 ♖g3

75...♔xa4?? allows 76 c7, when Black must even be creative to secure a draw: 76...♖b3+! 77 ♔c2 ♖xb5 78 c8♕ ♖c5+!! 79 ♕xc5 stalemate.

76 ♔c2 ♖g4 77 ♔b3 ♖b4+ 78 ♔c3 ♖b1 79 ♔c2 ♖f1 80 ♔b3 ♖a1!

At last White is in zugzwang.

81 ♔c4 ♖xa4+ 82 ♔c5 ♖a1 83 c7 ♖c1+ 84 ♔d6 ♔b6 0-1

As the pawns fall. To be fair to Colin, it was his desire to win earlier (a quality that gains him more points than it costs) that was his downfall in this game but praise should also go to Luke for his persistence in a position that at one time I would suspect that I would just 'give up'.

Endgame Exercises

In positions 1 to 6 the person to move has a fairly straightforward technical or tactical win. Position 7 requires that you analyse many variations to get to the truth of the situation. I suggest that to start with you try to judge who is better and why, as this may help lead you to the right course of action. Position 8 is more straightforward and depends on a small but very important finesse. Solutions are given on pages 134-7.

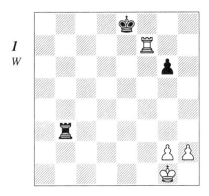

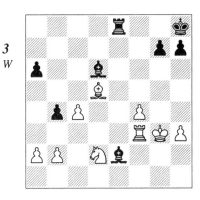

1
W

3
W

♖+2♙ vs ♖+♙ can be very tricky; what is the best way for White (to play) to finish it off?

White (to play) has been under pressure for some time. What is the best way for him now to clinch the draw?

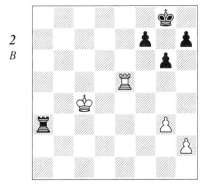

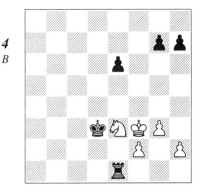

2
B

4
B

This time it's ♖+3♙ vs ♖+2♙. How does Black (to play) secure a win? There is a tactic in the main line that decides the issue.

Which is the simplest way for Black (to play) to realize his advantage?

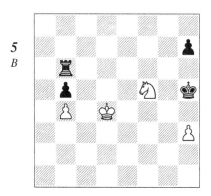

5
B

How can Black (to play) best make
progress? Keep in mind at a later stage
the theme involved in the previous example.

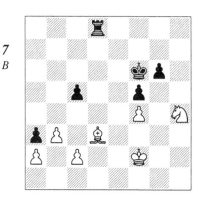

7
B

Black's position looks critical, but
how can he create active counterplay?

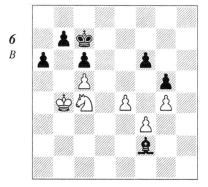

6
B

How should Black (to play) convert
his obvious advantage into victory?

8
W

White to play. Can he win?

4 Blunders and How to Avoid Them

First of all, let's ask ourselves what blunders are and what causes them. At the simplest level, a blunder is just a very bad move. However, we would normally only play such a move if there is something seemingly attractive about it – something that blinds us to the fatal flaw that renders the move so disastrous.

My advice here is that if you reach a position where the move you are contemplating seems very strong, then, before playing it, to spend a short period of time, up to a minute or two, contemplating your opponent's likely replies and immediate tactical possibilities. Sometimes in planning ahead long-range strategies and ideas you don't see the wood for the trees! There follow some examples of horrific errors, all taken from world championship matches.

In the following diagram, White, despite his nominal material advantage, must be careful of Black's passed a- and e-pawns. With the knight poorly placed on d8, my gut reaction would to bring it back into play. Obviously 57 ♘xb7?? allows 57...e2 winning, so 57 ♘e6+ seems natural and more or less forced without further analysis. White, however, decided to try to stop the e-pawn with his king and then to

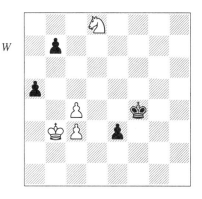

W

Bronstein – Botvinnik
Moscow Wch (6) 1951

stop Black's a-pawn with his knight, presumably with ♘xb7-c5-b3. Had he thought further he would have realized the error of his logic. After all, without the knight he would not be able to stop the e-pawn anyway, e.g. 57 ♔c2 ♔f3 58 ♔d1 ♔f2 followed by ...e2-e1♕. True, after 57 ♔c2 ♔f3 the knight could come back via e6 to d4 with check. However, that would not suit the purpose of trying to stop the e-pawn with the king and the a-pawn with the knight. So, apart from the problem shown by the game continuation, there was an error in the basic logic. At times, players tend to think more in moves than concepts. Whereas concrete analysis is at times vital, deciphering the logic of the position in terms of concepts is just as important. Often the correct solution can be found in a position without deep analysis.

57 ♔c2??

57 ♘e6+ ♔f3 58 ♘d4+ ♔f2 59 ♔a4 e2 60 ♘c2 (or 60 ♘xe2 ♔xe2 61 ♔xa5 ♔d3 drawing) 60...e1♕ 61 ♘xe1 ♔xe1 62 ♔xa5 ♔d2 63 ♔b4 b6! with a draw.

57...♔g3! *(D)*

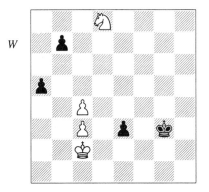

0-1

White resigned as the e-pawn promotes – 58 ♘e6 is now met by 58...e2 59 ♔d2 ♔f2. Was this a case of White just missing 57...♔g3! or getting the basic logic of the position wrong? I wonder if Bronstein had realized 57 ♘e6+ was 'just a draw' and therefore played 57 ♔c2 without too much thought as the obvious 'winning attempt'.

Our next example is far more trivial and demonstrates that the basic and disciplined habit of **considering all the opponent's checks and captures** would have saved the day.

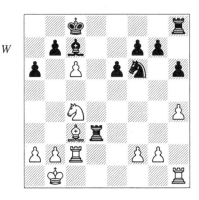

Smyslov – Botvinnik
Moscow Wch (3) 1958

28 ♘e5??

28 cxb7+ doesn't lead to much after 28...♔xb7 29 ♗e5 ♗xe5 30 ♘xe5 ♖d5 31 f4 ♘d7. 28 ♗e5 is probably best, when after 28...b5! (28...bxc6 29 ♗xc7 ♔xc7 30 ♘e5 ♖d5 31 ♘xc6 ♔d6 32 ♘b4 is good for White) 29 ♗xc7 ♔xc7 30 ♘e5 ♖d5 31 ♖e1 ♖f8 White's position is preferable although the final outcome is by no means certain.

28...♖xc3

White's position is now desperate. After 29 cxb7+ ♔xb7 30 ♖xc3 ♗xe5 Black had no problem capitalizing on his material advantage.

Our next position is another Botvinnik example but for once he is on the receiving end, this time at the hands of the 'Magician from Riga', Mikhail Tal.

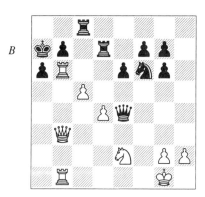

Tal – Botvinnik
Moscow Wch (17) 1960

Black is two pawns to the good and must obviously avoid 39...♕xe2??, when 40 ♖xb7+ ♚a8 41 ♖b8+ mates. Any counterplay White may generate is going to be based on 'cheapoes' against the black king and so a cautious move such as 39...♚a8 is called for, after which White is struggling for any play. Instead Black chose...

39...♕d5??

Logical in that it blockades White's d-pawn but again if Black had used the basic habit of considering all of White's checks and captures he would have spotted...

40 ♖xa6+ ♚b8

40...bxa6 41 ♕b6+ ♚a8 42 ♕xa6+ ♖a7 43 ♕xc8#.

41 ♕a4 1-0

Black resigned as he cannot parry the threats.

Not all of our examples involve Botvinnik though! Our next example features the two men who, between

them, held the world title from 1963 to 1972.

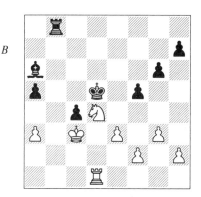

Petrosian – Spassky
Moscow Wch (14) 1969

Optically White looks better due to his superior pawn-structure and well-placed knight on d4 compared to Black's light-squared bishop on a6. However, Black's control of the b-file evens things up and after 43...♚c5 it is difficult to see the game ending in anything but a draw. However, Black has other ideas...

43...♚e4?? 44 f3+! ♚xe3 45 ♖d2

Petrosian plays for mate! The only amazing thing about this position now is that after the more or less forced **45...♖b3+** Black still managed to draw!

Next one of the most famous 'blunders' of all time (*see diagram on following page*).

Most people were now expecting a 'quick handshake' between the players to agree the draw. What follows is

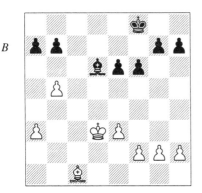

Spassky – Fischer
Reykjavik Wch (1) 1972

probably a miscalculation, with Fischer presumably missing 35 ♗d2 in the note to Black's 32nd move. One thing that should be remembered is that although Fischer was strong favourite to win the match based on rating and his form at the time, he had never as yet beaten Spassky in a game!

29...♗xh2??

Grabbing a rook's pawn like this is often an error, but one should always be on the lookout for exceptions to the 'rules'. Strictly speaking this move may not be losing, as exhaustive analysis has shown that on best play Black may yet be able to hold the resulting position. However, the move still deserves a '??' on the grounds that before it the position should have been trivially drawn and now Black needs to find an exact defence, which he failed to do over the board.

30 g3 h5 31 ♔e2 h4 32 ♔f3 hxg3

After the alternative 32...h3, White continues 33 ♔g4 ♗g1 34 ♔xh3 ♗xf2

35 ♗d2 and Black's bishop remains trapped.

33 fxg3 ♔e7 34 ♔g2

White eventually won.

We now move on to the 1980s, and a couple of examples involving the two players who dominated the chess world in that decade.

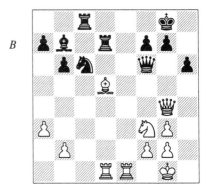

Kasparov – Karpov
Moscow Wch (11) 1985

22...♖cd8??

Black's position is by no means as comfortable as you might suspect, as the following variations show:

a) 22...♖e7? 23 ♖xe7 ♕xe7 24 ♗xf7+! ♕xf7 25 ♖d7 h5 26 ♕h3 and White is well on top.

b) 22...♖dc7 and 22...♖dd8 are little better, as 23 b4! keeps Black under extreme pressure.

c) 22...♖d6! is the best defence, trying to neutralize White's active pieces. For example, 23 ♖e4 (23 ♗e4 ♖cd8 24 ♖xd6 ♖xd6 25 b4 ♖e6! and Black has a comfortable position)

23...♖f8! (protecting his weak point at f7) 24 ♖f4 ♕d8 25 ♕h5 ♘e5!.

23 ♕xd7! ♖xd7 24 ♖e8+ ♔h7 25 ♗e4+ 1-0

After 25...g6 26 ♖xd7 ♗a6 27 ♗xc6 White wins a further piece.

I have some sympathy with Karpov here as he was under a great deal of pressure in the original position and 22...♖cd8 seems a natural response; indeed, had it not been for White's tactical response, 22...♖cd8 may well have been the strongest reply. Once again (maybe I should shout it from the rooftops!) consider **all** your opponent's checks **and** captures.

Our final example from world championship play features a number of blunders, inaccuracies and misjudgements from both sides.

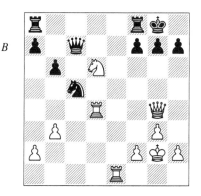

Kasparov – Karpov
Moscow Wch (16) 1984/5

White is better due to his knight on d6 and more active rooks but the advantage is by no means conclusive.

22...♘e6?? 23 ♖xe6!

Black's last move was asking for trouble.

23...h5!

After 23...fxe6 24 ♕xe6+ ♔h8 25 ♖c4! Black can no longer cover f7.

24 ♕e4 fxe6 25 ♕xe6+ ♔h7 26 ♖d5?

White should have played 26 ♖c4! ♕d8 27 ♕e4+ ♔h8 (27...g6 28 ♕b7+ ♔g8 29 ♖c7 wins) 28 ♕e5 and Black can pack his bags.

26...g6 27 ♘e4 ♖ad8 28 ♘g5+ ♔g7 29 ♕e4 ♖fe8 30 ♕d4+?

After 30 ♘e6+ ♖xe6 31 ♕d4+ (not 31 ♕xe6?? ♕b7, when it is Black who is winning) White comes out a pawn ahead but still with a number of technical difficulties if he is to convert the position into a full point.

30...♔g8 31 ♖xd8??

31 ♕f6! secures the draw after 31...♖xd5 32 ♕xg6+ ♔f8 33 ♕f6+, etc.

31...♖xd8 32 ♕f6 ♖d6

Now, all of a sudden, it is Black who is better.

Coming back down to earth, let us look at an example between 'us mortals'.

Keely – D. Parr
Hastings Challengers 1998/9

1 e4 c5 2 ♘f3 d6 3 d4 cxd4 4 ♘xd4 ♘f6 5 ♘c3 g6 6 f4

This system was originally designed to meet 6...♗g7 with 7 e5!?; for example, 7...dxe5 8 fxe5 ♘h5?! 9 ♗b5+ ♔f8?? 10 ♘e6+. Nowadays,

Black is generally wise to this and thus 6 f4 loses its bite.

6...♘c6 7 ♘xc6 bxc6 8 e5 dxe5

An immediate 8...♘d7 may well be better.

9 ♕xd8+ ♔xd8 10 fxe5 ♘g4

10...♘d5 is Black's main alternative.

11 ♗f4 ♗g7 12 ♖d1+ ♔e8?? 13 ♘b5! 1-0

Black resigned in view of 13...cxb5 (13...♖b8 14 ♘c7+ ♔f8 15 ♖d8#) 14 ♗xb5+ ♗d7 (14...♔f8 15 ♖d8#) 15 ♗xd7+ ♔f8 16 ♗xg4.

This just goes to show you need to know your systems well, especially the slightly unusual but potentially dangerous lines.

One of the things that amazes me is how even a very strong player can see the potential dangers in a position and then still allow the same winning concept. Here is an example (*see following diagram*):

The position is full of tactics, which mostly favour Black. I would suspect that Chris Ward was already short of time; he now falls headlong into Black's main tactical concept.

19 ♗e3??

After 19 ♖xe8? f2+ 20 ♔h1 ♖axe8 (but not 20...f1♕+?? 21 ♖xf1, when the f8-rook is pinned) White is helpless to stop the threats. White must have seen this and should have put up

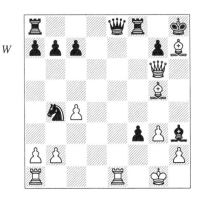

Ward – Bellin
British League (4NCL) 1996/7

stubborn resistance by means of 19 ♗f4!, when Black has no clear route to victory.

19...♕xe3+! 0-1

White resigned in view of 20 ♖xe3 f2+ 21 ♔h1 f1♕+ 22 ♖xf1 ♖xf1#. I'm sure Robert Bellin got a lot of pleasure out of that one.

One of the greatest pleasures for me in playing through a section such as this is to see how even some of the greatest players of all time are human, and capable of the most outrageous howlers! It gives us all hope and comfort in the knowledge when we commit something as 'grim' that tomorrow is another day and one in which we can again attempt to prove ourselves great as well.

5 How to Play against Much Weaker Opponents

Not surprisingly, the technique is generally the opposite to that when you are playing much stronger opposition (which is discussed in the next chapter) – in other words, avoid unnecessary complications, unless you are certain of the outcome, and try to keep things well under control. Often it is not necessary to have a distinct advantage as the cumulative pressure usually tells. Our first example is one of my own from the Bristol League. My opponent, whilst experienced and by no means anybody's fool, chose a line that could at best be described as unadventurous.

Baker – Collier
Bristol League 1997/8

1 e4 c5 2 ᐁc3

A useful move-order to avoid the main-line Najdorf, a favourite of my opponent here.

2...ᐁc6 3 ᐁf3 e6 4 d4 cxd4 5 ᐁxd4 a6 6 ᐁxc6 dxc6?

Whilst not as obviously wrong as a move that drops a pawn, this move is no less a blunder in my opinion, as it condemns Black to a prospectless middlegame. Of course, 6...bxc6 would be the standard move.

7 ᐁxd8+ ⬕xd8 8 ᘓf4

To my logic White can already claim a significant advantage: he has a lead in development, Black's pawn-structure on the queenside is riddled with dark-squared weaknesses and as yet his king hasn't found long-term sanctuary.

8...b5 9 0-0-0+ ⬕e8 10 ᘓd6!

This move and its follow-up took considerable thought but in reality the exchange of the dark-squared bishops only heightens Black's weaknesses.

10...ᐁf6 11 ᘓe2! *(D)*

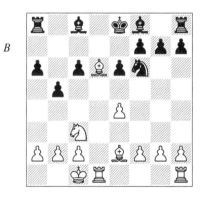

The move White wanted to play and one of the few during the game that needed tactical justification.

11...ᘓa7

After 11...b4 12 ᐁa4 ᘓxd6 (the alternative 12...ᐁxe4 13 ᘓxf8 ᘓxf8 14

♗f3 f5 15 ♘c5! ♖a7 16 ♘xe4 fxe4 17 ♗xe4 ♖xf2 18 ♗xc6+ ♗d7 19 ♖xd7 ♖xd7 20 ♖d1 ♖ff7 21 ♖d6! is very strong for White) 13 ♖xd6 ♘xe4 14 ♖d4 ♘xf2 (14...f5 15 ♗f3 ♖f8 16 ♘c5! e5 17 ♖xb4 and again Black has problems) 15 ♖f1 e5 16 ♖h4! g5 (after 16...♘g4? 17 ♘b6 White emerges material up) 17 ♖xb4 a5 18 ♖c4 ♗a6 19 ♖c5 ♗xe2 20 ♖xe5+ ♔f8 21 ♖xf2 ♗b5 22 ♘c5 Black has big problems.

12 e5 ♘d5 13 ♘e4 h5 14 h4!

Stopping any chances of activity or space-gaining by Black.

14...f5 15 ♗xf8 ♔xf8 16 ♘c5 ♔e7 17 g3 ♘b6?

Removing Black's only good piece from its outpost while allowing a white rook to penetrate.

18 ♖d6 ♖c7 19 ♖hd1 g6 20 b3

White's task of restricting Black to passivity while improving his own pieces is near completion.

20...♘d5 21 ♔b2! *(D)*

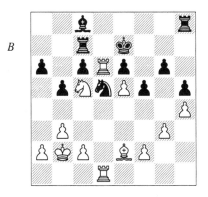

Preparing, amongst other things, c2-c4 kicking away Black's knight from its one-time secure outpost.

21...a5 22 c4

White now has an enormous advantage.

22...bxc4 23 bxc4 ♘b4

If we compare pawn-structures together with the fact that it is difficult to find one of Black's pieces that is better than its counterpart, it is not surprising that he is on the edge of a precipice.

24 ♗f3 ♖f8 25 a3 ♘a6 *(D)*

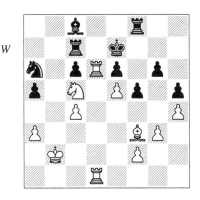

26 ♘d3!

No way am I going to allow the exchange of those knights! Mine is destined for better things – firstly restricting Black from playing ...f4 but more importantly occupying that juicy f4-square.

26...c5 27 ♘f4 ♔f7 *(D)*

28 ♖b6!

Preparing to double up rooks on the sixth rank. This is enough to decide the issue.

28...♖e8 29 ♖dd6 ♖ee7 30 ♖xa6 ♗xa6 31 ♖xa6 ♖cd7 32 ♔c3

Stopping any chance of Black immediately doubling rooks on the d-file.

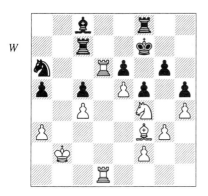

W

32...罝d4 33 罝xa5 罝ed7 34 罝xc5 罝d2 35 奧d5! 1-0

A final accurate touch to complete the demolition. From my perspective this was a very satisfying encounter.

When facing a much stronger opponent, many players are tempted to try something surprising in the opening. This may arise from a belief that the stronger player's opening knowledge is a major factor in his higher rating, and that this erudition must be avoided at all cost ("I wanted to get you out of your book" is often heard in post-mortem analysis as the justification for a poor move in the opening). This often takes the form of an unsound system, or a speculative gambit. However, this often just plays into the hands of the stronger player. Assuming we do not panic, or take inappropriate risks in an all-out attempt to refute the opponent's play, we should be able to steer the game into an unbalanced (or simply superior) position where our (presumably) superior play should enable us to win through. The next two

games are good examples of how to deal with an opening surprise by your opponent.

Baker – J. Turner
Monmouth 1997

1 e4 e5 2 ♘f3 d5!? 3 ♘xe5

This, as I knew, was by no means the critical test of 2...d5!? but my recommended policy when unexpectedly encountering something unusual is to avoid critical lines, especially when they involve messy tactical variations for which the opponent is undoubtedly well prepared. In this way, while you may not get a 'normal' theoretical edge, you can at least expect a reasonable position from which you will still have the opportunity to play chess and try to outplay the opponent.

3...dxe4?!

This is unusual. I was anticipating 3...♗d6.

4 d4

While I thought 4 ♗c4 may well be right, I continued with my previous policy.

4...♗d6 5 ♘c4 ♘f6

5...♗e7, preserving the bishop, has been played before and may well be best.

6 ♘xd6+ cxd6

I was expecting 6...♕xd6.

7 ♗e2 0-0 8 0-0 罝e8 9 ♘c3 a6?

This move is wrong as the plan of ...b5 turns out badly. Some sort of natural developing move was called for but I was expecting errors, as my opponent was having to think for himself!

10 ♗g5

By now I was starting to feel quite comfortable with the bishop-pair and a slight lead in development. Moreover, I was happy that we were well and truly out of *his* book!

10...b5 11 f3! *(D)*

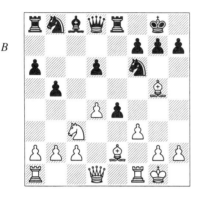

A strong move as it wipes away one of Black's trump cards – his strong e-pawn. This idea seemed consistent with the equivalent idea in some lines of the Latvian Gambit.

11...exf3

After 11...e3?! 12 ♕d3 h6 13 ♗xe3 ♕e7 14 ♗f2! b4 15 ♘e4 ♘xe4 16 fxe4 ♗b7 (16...♕xe4? 17 ♕xe4 ♖xe4 18 ♗f3 wins the exchange) 17 ♗f3 ♗xe4 18 ♗xe4 ♕xe4 19 ♖ae1 ♕c6 (not 19...♕xd3?? 20 ♖xe8+) 20 d5 ♕d7 21 ♗d4 White has a very comfortable position.

However, 11...d5! is almost certainly the critical test of White's last move. After 12 ♗xf6 gxf6 13 ♕e1! White has a long-term edge due to the plan of f4, ♘d1-e3, c3 and play on the kingside. This seems clearer than 13

fxe4 dxe4 14 ♘xe4!? ♖xe4 15 ♗f3 ♖xd4 16 ♕e1 ♖a7 17 ♕g3+ ♔h8 18 ♕xb8, although this may be just a matter of taste.

12 ♗xf3 ♖a7 13 ♘e4?!

13 ♘d5 may well be more accurate.

13...♖e6?

13...♗f5 is a better try.

14 ♘xf6+ gxf6 15 ♗h4 d5 16 ♕d2 ♘c6 17 ♗g4 ♖d6 18 ♗xc8 ♕xc8 19 ♕f4 ♕d8 20 ♖ae1!

Admittedly 20 ♗xf6 would have won the exchange and a pawn, but I saw no need to 'sell myself cheaply'.

20...♖e7 21 ♗xf6!

Now there is a sting in the tail.

21...♖xf6 22 ♕xf6 ♖xe1 23 ♕xf7+ ♔h8 24 ♖xe1 1-0

Baker – Horton-Kitchen
Newport Open 1999

1 e4 e5 2 ♘f3 ♘c6 3 ♗c4 d6?!

I regard this as 'solid'. However, if Black intends ...♗e7 and ...♘f6 transposing back to normal lines then fair enough, although this move-order appears to offer less flexibility. I knew 4 c3 and 4 d4 were regarded as the critical lines but I had another, 'safer', idea in mind.

4 d3 ♗g4

I was quite happy for Black to transpose, as suggested in the previous note, back into the systems I feel most comfortable with.

5 h3 ♗xf3!? 6 ♕xf3 ♕f6 7 ♕g3 ♘a5!?

I must admit that I was expecting 7...♕g6 8 ♕xg6 hxg6 9 c3, when I hoped that my bishop-pair and Black's weak point at f7 would provide me with an edge.

8 ♗b5+ c6 9 ♗a4 b5 10 ♗d2 ♘b7

10...♕d8 seems like a sensible alternative.

11 ♗b3 ♘c5 12 ♗e3!

My bishop was doing nothing on d2 and I wanted to keep that square as an option for my knight while trying to force Black into making a decision.

12...♘xb3 13 axb3 a6 14 0-0 *(D)*

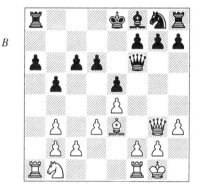

14...♕e6?! 15 ♘c3 ♘f6 16 ♖a5!

Tying down the potential weakness on a6.

16...g6 17 ♖fa1 ♕c8 18 d4

18 ♘a2 followed by ♘b4 seems like a good option as well but I wanted to put on as much pressure as possible.

18...♘d7 19 d5!

Now Black is struggling.

19...♗g7 20 dxc6 ♕xc6 21 ♘xb5

I wanted to play 21 ♘d5 but was not convinced by the line 21...♕xc2 22 ♖c1 ♕xe4 23 ♘c7+ ♔e7 24 ♘xa8 ♖xa8.

21...0-0 22 ♘c3 ♔h8 23 ♕f3 f5 24 exf5! ♕c8

24...♕xf3?! 25 gxf3 ♖xf5 26 ♖xa6 ♖xa6 27 ♖xa6 is hardly attractive.

25 f6!

I didn't want him to get any active counterplay with a later ...gxf5.

25...♘xf6 26 ♕e2 ♕d7 27 ♖xa6 ♖xa6 28 ♖xa6! d5 29 ♗c5 ♖e8 30 ♕b5!

Queens off please!

30...♖c8 31 ♕xd7 ♘xd7 32 b4! d4

32...♘xc5 33 bxc5 ♖xc5?? 34 ♖a8+ wins a piece.

33 ♘e4 ♔g8 34 ♖d6 ♖c7 35 c3!

Aimed at 'straightening out' my pawns as well as getting rid of Black's passed pawn.

35...♘xc5 36 bxc5 dxc3 37 bxc3

Part A of my plan had failed but now I have a strong passed pawn on c5, the superior kingside structure, the better minor piece and am under no pressure whatsoever. The rest, as they say, was just technique.

Miles – G. Wall
British League (4NCL) 1998/9

1 c4 g6 2 e4 e5 3 d4 ♘f6

Black's opening looks rather odd to me, but is actually considered quite respectable, and fits in with the idea of aiming for a mess against the stronger player.

4 ♘f3 ♘xe4

This leads to trouble. 4...♗b4+ is normal, while 4...exd4 is also possible.

5 ♗d3 ♗b4+ 6 ♔f1!

White doesn't worry about misplacing his king but instead tries to show how the black pieces are out on a limb.

6...d5 *(D)*

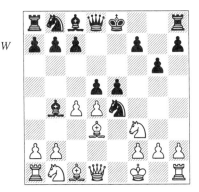

7 ♕b3!!

7 ♘xe5 0-0 8 f3 had previously been played in the game Ubilava-Sion Castro, Ampuriabrava 1997, which White went on to win, although not totally convincingly. The text-move is an excellent way to make sense of the position. The alternative 7 ♕a4+ ♘c6 8 ♘xe5 ♘xf2 leads to very messy positions:

a) 9 ♘xc6 bxc6 10 ♕xc6+ (the continuation 10 ♔xf2 ♕f6+ 11 ♔e3 ♕e6+ 12 ♔f2 ♕f6+ is a good way to take a draw) 10...♗d7 11 ♕xd5 ♘xd3 12 ♕e4+ ♗e6 13 ♕xd3 ♕f6+ 14 ♔g1 and Black has some activity/lead in development in compensation for the pawn.

b) 9 ♔xf2 ♕h4+ 10 ♔f3 ♕xd4 is not so clear and would have been just

the kind of idea and position Black had been hoping for.

7...c5

7...dxc4?! 8 ♕xc4 ♘f6 9 ♕xb4 e4 10 ♕e1 ♕e7 11 ♗g5! is very strong for White, while 7...a5 8 a3 ♗e7 (8...dxc4? 9 ♗xc4 ♗d6 10 ♗xf7+ is grim) 9 cxd5 ♘f6 10 ♗b5+ ♗d7 11 dxe5 is no better than the game.

8 cxd5 ♘f6 9 dxe5

The immediate 9 ♗g5 is an attractive alternative.

9...♘xd5 10 ♗g5 ♕d7 11 a3 b5

After 11...♗a5 12 ♘bd2 ♗xd2 (after 12...♘c6, 13 ♘e4 threatening ♕xd5 followed by ♘f6+ is very strong) 13 ♘xd2 White's massive lead in development, together with Black's dark-squared weaknesses, leaves him with a commanding position.

12 ♗e4 c4 13 ♕c2 ♗a5

13...♗c5? 14 ♘c3 wins material in a similar fashion to the game.

14 ♘c3! ♗xc3?

After a difficult defence Black finally succumbs. 14...♗b7! is Black's best try as 15 ♖d1 ♗xc3 16 bxc3 ♘a6 is not conclusive, although White still enjoys an edge.

15 ♗xd5 1-0

Winning a piece as 15...♕xd5 16 ♖d1, and ♖d8# if Black saves his queen, is decisive. An excellent performance by Tony Miles which shows he has lost none of his 'touch'.

6 How to Play against Much Stronger Opponents

I am not going to pretend that there is some magic way to beat players who are stronger than you. However, by adopting the right approach to encounters with strong players, it is possible to make sure you get all the points you deserve (and hopefully a few that you don't!). At the very least, we can make sure we don't get crushed like a bug – they will have to prove that they are good players!

How to tackle these games depends very much on 'any other' factors. By this I mean if the stronger player needs to win almost at any cost, since, for example, he is half a point behind in the tournament or he needs to win for his team. Other things being equal, I think it is a case of 'judging' your opponent's style.

Against a strong player who likes to maintain control, even if it means he keeps only a minimal edge, I would recommend that you opt for an unclear position where the player who makes the first slip is likely to fall off the edge of the precipice. Admittedly it is more likely to be the weaker player who falls, but at least you have the chance that he will err – and should he do so, it will be fatal. On the other hand, if you aim for a minimal disadvantage it leaves the stronger player

with the comfortable feeling that he can carry on without risk. This offers him chances of 'grinding it out'. Moreover, if he makes an inaccuracy it may be of such a subtle nature that you don't pick up on it, or that even if you do, you are still no better than equal, leaving him the opportunity of outplaying you all over again.

The alternative technique, most likely to be appropriate if you are White, is to play a tight system which, while it may be academically reasonable for your opponent, requires him to play with great accuracy. The drawback of this is that if your opponent plays well, then he may well reach the type of position where he can start grinding. However, the results if he goes wrong can be quite spectacular providing you have the courage of your convictions (see S.Buckley-Baker later in this section).

Let us look at some examples of 'giant-killing'.

Baker – King
British League (4NCL) 1997/8

1 e4 c5 2 ♘c3 d6 3 f4

Due to Black's move-order (2...d6, rather than 2...♘c6 or 2...e6) White can enter a Grand Prix Attack without meeting ...e6 and ...d5 variations or some of the critical variations involving ...g6.

3...♘c6 4 ♘f3 g6 5 ♗b5 ♗d7 6 0-0 ♗g7 7 d3 a6 8 ♗xc6 ♗xc6 9 ♔h1

White plans, should Black castle quickly on the kingside, to play ♕e1-h4, f5 and ♗h6, etc.

9...♕d7!?

Black tries to maintain flexibility on which side to castle.

10 ♕e1 ♘h6 11 ♗d2 f5 12 ♘d5!? (D)

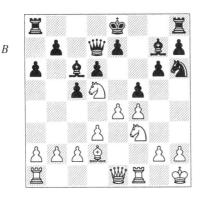

B

Objectively this may not be best but it requires Black to commit himself in some way.

12...fxe4

12...♗xd5 13 exd5 (13 ♗c3?! fxe4 14 ♗xg7? exf3! is winning for Black) 13...♗xb2 14 ♖b1 ♗f6 15 ♘g5 ♗xg5 16 fxg5 ♘f7 17 ♕e6 ♕xe6 18 dxe6 ♘d8 19 ♖b6 leaves White with quite a bind for the pawn. Also it was difficult for Black to judge whether White had anything better along the way – not the kind of decision and commitment Black wanted to make.

Alternatively, 12...♗xb2?! 13 ♘b6 ♕d8 14 ♘xa8 ♗xa1 15 ♕xa1 0-0 16 ♕e1! ♕xa8 17 ♕h4 leaves White with excellent chances.

13 ♕xe4 ♘f7

13...e6?! is somewhat dubious. Moreover, it allows White to create the type of mess he has been aiming for: 14 ♖ae1 0-0 (14...♔f8? 15 ♘b6 ♕d8 16 ♕xe6! ♕xb6 and now 17 f5! wins in all variations) 15 ♘b6 with an edge for White.

14 ♖ae1 ♗xd5 15 ♕xd5 0-0

Black picks the correct moment to bail out. Alternatives are no better, e.g. 15...♗xb2? 16 ♖b1 e6 17 ♖fe1 0-0-0 18 ♖xe6 ♗g7 19 ♗a5 and Black is in deep trouble.

16 ♘g5!

Turning the screws.

16...♕c6

16...♗xb2 17 ♖b1 ♗f6 18 ♖xb7 ♕a4 19 ♘e6 ♖fb8 20 ♖b3! leaves White with a pleasant edge.

17 ♕xc6 bxc6 18 ♘e6 ♖fb8 19 ♘xg7 ♔xg7 20 f5!

The greedy move 20 ♖xe7? allows 20...♔f8!, when Black has turned the tables.

20...gxf5 21 ♖xe7 ♖e8?!

21...♔f8! was Black's last chance to play for activity. However, with time-trouble looming he opts to go solid.

21...♖xb2?? allows 22 ♗c3+ ♔f8 23 ♖xf7+ ♔xf7 24 ♗xb2.

22 ♗c3+ ♔g6 23 ♖fe1! ♘e5 24 ♖c7 (D)

24...♖e6? 25 ♖xc6 ♖ae8 26 ♖xa6 ♘g4? 27 ♖xd6

Three moves and three pawns – not bad for a hacker!

27...Rxd6 28 Rxe8

The rest of the game was played by inertia by Black to reach the time-control.

28...c4 29 h3 cxd3 30 Rg8+ Kf7 31 Rg7+ Ke6 32 cxd3

32 hxg4?? dxc2 was the last chance for White to mess it up.

32...Nf2+ 33 Kg1 Nxd3 34 Rxh7 Kd5 35 Rf7 f4 36 Kf1 Re6 37 a4 Ke4 38 a5 Ke3 39 Rf6 Re4 40 a6 Ra4 41 Re6+

Finally, it falls apart completely.

1-0

The second example is one where I am on the receiving end. I'm not proud of it, but credit where credit is due.

S. Buckley – Baker
Newport 1999

1 e4 c6 2 d4 g6 3 Nc3 Bg7 4 Nf3 d6 5 Be3 b5 6 Bd3 a6?!

It may well have been better to get on with things with normal developing moves, retaining the option of meeting a4 at some stage with ...b4 and ...a5.

This would gain a tempo over later possibilities where Black plays ...b4 and ...a5. However, at the time I wanted to adopt a 'wait and see' approach.

7 Qd2 Nd7 8 0-0 e5?

Black needed to prepare this central advance first with moves like ...Ngf6, ...0-0 and ...Qc7, when he would have reached a sensible set-up.

9 dxe5 dxe5 10 a4! *(D)*

Now Black has no adequate way of meeting this move because 10...Rb8 11 axb5 axb5 12 Ra7 leaves White with a pleasant advantage and, as previously mentioned, playing 10...b4 and ...a5 would mean losing a valuable tempo.

10...Bb7 11 axb5 axb5 12 Rxa8 Bxa8

12...Qxa8 is even worse due to 13 Bxb5! cxb5 14 Nxb5 Qb8 15 Ba7!, winning outright.

13 Nxb5!! *(D)*

It was the sheer power of this move that I had missed. I think Black is now busted.

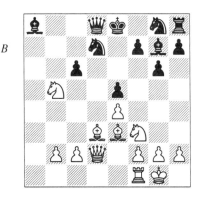

13...cxb5 14 ♗xb5 ♘e7

14...♗xe4 may have been a better try although after 15 ♘g5! ♗f5 16 ♕d5 ♘h6 17 ♖d1 ♕c7 18 ♗c5! Black seems totally stifled.

15 ♕d6 ♘c8

15...♗xe4? 16 ♘xe5 ♗f5 17 ♘xd7 ♗xd7 18 ♖d1 finishes things off. It may have been the correct time to give back the material by 15...0-0, although then Black's position is still rocky to say the least. To be honest though, by now I was already 'punch-drunk' and had totally missed White's reply to the text-move.

16 ♕b8!

I had only considered 16 ♕a6, when 16...♗xe4 gives White problems in justifying his piece sacrifice.

16...♗xe4 17 ♘xe5! ♘cb6?!

Obviously 17...♗xe5?? is hopeless after 18 ♕xe5+. 17...♔e7!? is an option, although after 18 ♗xd7 ♘d6 19 ♘c6+ ♗xc6 20 ♕xd8+ ♖xd8 21 ♗xc6 ♗xb2 22 ♗g5+ f6 23 ♖e1+ ♔f7 24 ♗d5+ ♔g7 25 ♗f4, with all his pluses, White should have little problem converting his advantage into victory.

18 ♕d6 ♕e7 19 ♕b8+ ♕d8 20 ♕xd8+! ♔xd8 21 ♘xf7+ ♔c7

21...♔e7 22 ♘xh8 ♔f8 23 ♖e1 ♗xc2 24 ♗xb6 ♘xb6 25 ♖e8# would have been an attractive and perhaps fitting way for the game to finish.

22 ♗f4+ ♔b7 23 ♘d6+ ♔b8 24 ♘xe4+ ♘e5 25 ♘c5 1-0

The following game shows how even a strong grandmaster such as Mark Hebden can misjudge the tactical implications of a position at times.

Marusenko – Hebden
Hastings Challengers 1998/9

1 e4 e5 2 ♘f3 ♘c6 3 ♗c4 ♘f6 4 ♘g5 d5 5 exd5 ♘a5 6 ♗b5+ c6 7 dxc6 bxc6 8 ♗d3!?

This is relatively unusual, with 8 ♗e2 or occasionally 8 ♕f3 being 'normal'. The only other example of the text-move I could find was Marusenko-Fox, Hastings Challengers 1994/5 and so I must assume it is a Marusenko speciality.

8...♗c5 9 0-0 0-0 10 ♘c3 ♗b6 11 b4!

This seems the most logical way to exploit Black's last move in that it not only gains time on the black knight but also offers a route out for White's dark-squared bishop, which was previously hemmed in.

11...♘b7 12 ♕f3 h6 13 ♘ge4 ♘d5 14 b5!

Black's compensation for the pawn seems rather nebulous to me. This queenside thrust, while potentially removing one of Black's weaknesses, undermines Black's support for his central d5-knight.

14...♞xc3

14...cxb5?? 15 ♞xd5 wins material as 15...♛xd5?? loses the queen to 16 ♞f6+.

15 dxc3 f5 16 ♗a3!! *(D)*

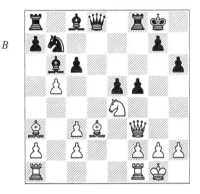

I suspect Hebden had missed this move.

16...♞a5

16...fxe4?? 17 ♗c4+ wins the rook on f8.

17 ♗xf8 fxe4?

17...♛xf8! 18 bxc6 fxe4 19 ♛xf8+ ♚xf8 20 ♗xe4 ♗e6 leaves White with a much harder task despite his material advantage and Black's temporary lack of piece coordination. In fact, the potential of Black's pieces may well leave him with excellent practical chances and so the text-move must have just been based on a miscalculation or a total oversight.

18 ♗xe4 ♛xf8?? 19 ♗h7+ ♚xh7 20 ♛xf8

Black might have well have resigned here.

The story doesn't end there. Hebden got to play Black against Marusenko within a few days in the Hastings weekend tournament and had his revenge with 6...♗d7 in the same opening. This is an excellent example of 'temporary repairs' to your opening repertoire until you have the time, if possible, to improve on a set-back and plug the gap.

To show this is no fluke, look at how another strong grandmaster bites the dust when, after being under pressure for some time, he finally cracks.

Burgess – Chandler
British League (4NCL) 1996/7

1 d4 d5 2 c4 e6 3 ♞c3 c5 4 cxd5 exd5 5 ♞f3 ♞c6 6 g3 ♞f6 7 ♗g2 ♗e7 8 0-0 0-0 9 ♗g5 cxd4 10 ♞xd4 h6 11 ♗e3 ♖e8 12 ♛b3 ♞a5 13 ♛c2 ♗g4 14 ♞f5 ♗b4 15 ♗d4 ♗xc3 16 ♗xc3 ♞c4

After a lot of theory in one of Murray's favourite defences, White now plays a new move, offering a pawn in return for pressure.

17 h3 ♗xf5 18 ♛xf5 ♖xe2

18...d4?! 19 ♖ad1 ♞d6 20 ♛f4 dxc3 21 ♖xd6 ♛e7 (after 21...♛a5 22 bxc3, despite his loose pawns, White is likely to emerge on top; for example, 22...♖ac8 23 ♗xb7 ♖xc3 24 ♗c6!) 22 bxc3 ♛xe2 23 ♗xb7 favours White.

19 ♗f3!? *(D)*

Removing the enemy rook from the seventh.

19...♖e6 20 ♖ad1 ♞d6!

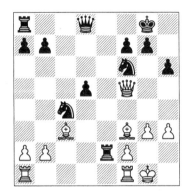

20...♘b6!?, while not very appealing, would hold on to the extra pawn for the time being, and put the onus on White to turn his advantages into something concrete.

21 ♗xf6 ♖xf6

After 21...♘xf5! 22 ♗xd8 ♖xd8 23 ♖xd5 the game may well peter out to a draw. However, the 'much stronger player' evidently wants more, as the resulting position would offer very few chances to gain an advantage. He therefore plays so as to complicate matters.

22 ♕xd5 ♕b6 23 ♖d2 ♖c8

Compare this position with the one that occurs just seven moves later to see how things change so quickly.

24 ♖fd1 ♖c5 25 ♕d4 ♕c7 26 ♔g2 a5 27 a3 b5 28 ♖e2!

Aiming to occupy the more valuable e-file.

28...a4 29 ♖e5 ♖c2 30 ♖de1 *(D)*

White maintains a pleasant edge due to his superior minor piece, control of the e-file, well-placed queen and safer king.

30...♘f5?? 31 ♖xf5!

Exploiting the fact that Black's bolt-hole for his king is on the same colour square as White's bishop.

31...♖xf5 32 ♖e8+ ♔h7 33 ♗e4 ♖c5

Unfortunately 33...g6??, the natural way of returning the exchange, allows mate on h8 while exchanging queens by 33...♕c5 34 ♕xc5 ♖xc5 35 g4 is also hopeless.

34 g4 ♕f4 35 ♕e3!

White forces a queen exchange, so reducing the chance of 'accidents'.

35...♕xe3 36 fxe3 g6 37 gxf5

The rest, as they say, is just technique.

Hebden normally performs excellently against weaker players but here *(see next diagram)* his Scandinavian Gambit (1 e4 d5 2 exd5 ♘f6 3 d4 ♗g4!?) has gone wrong and in persisting in being aggressive he runs into an excellent counter-attack:

Black had just played the over-optimistic 16...g7-g5?, which White now despatched mercilessly.

17 d5!!

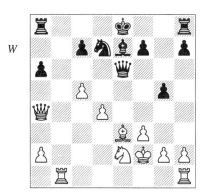

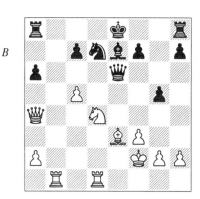

C. Cobb – Hebden
British League (4NCL) 1997/8

Timed to perfection. White gives up a pawn to open the d-file with devastating effect.

17...♕xd5 18 ♖hd1 ♕e6 19 ♘d4 *(D)*

Just compare the white pieces with their black counterparts and you can appreciate Black's problems. In the end, the comparative placements of the kings decides the issue.

19...♕g6 20 ♘c6!

The huge threat of ♖xd7 followed by ♘e5++, or the more mundane ♘e5, leaves Black without resource.

20...♗xc5 21 ♘e5 ♗xe3+ 22 ♔xe3

Rarely has a king on the third rank in an open position with all the major pieces still on the board looked so secure.

22...♕e6 23 ♕xd7+ ♕xd7 24 ♘xd7

Black could now have quite easily considered resigning.

Part 2: During the Game

After the hard work of Part 1, in this section of the book I shall be taking a look at some aspects of conduct at the board. I hope these observations will be useful in both adding to your enjoyment of competitive play, and to helping you score as many points as possible.

While rereading this part of the book, I realized that the thing I am most guilty of myself is 'wandering off' from the board too often for a 'quick cigarette'. I may kid myself that this is to relax and reduce stress, but the breaks in my concentration and the breaking of my train of thought cannot be good for my game. Maybe you will also recognize characteristic failings of your own, and if so, you will already have taken the first step towards correcting them.

Knowing the rules of the game is important as much as a means of self-preservation as anything else. One should play the game in the right spirit, but draw the line at being treated like a mug! You really ought to know how to claim what is rightly yours, e.g. threefold repetition. The rules have changed in recent years, and not knowing how to make the claim is just careless and causes self-recrimination.

Good clock-handling is a vital ingredient in successful play, and Chapter 9 provides some advice on how to put your precious time to good use. I promised myself never to get into serious time-trouble without due cause ever since I lost to my brother on time in the Coventry League in 1973, and so try to use my time wisely; after all, time is money and I have little of either!

One should always be courteous towards one's opponent, other players and the arbiters – this minimizes the likelihood of serious disputes and should make your chess-playing a more pleasant experience. In Chapter 7, I discuss behaviour on and off the board, and provide some advice on what to do on the rare occasions when an opponent behaves improperly.

I must admit, though, that of the chapters within Part 2, none brings such a glow or a warm feeling to the stomach as Chapter 10, Swindling Your Opponent. There is nothing so decadent as taking away from your opponent what he may regard as rightfully his – I cannot help but feel a little guilty when I seize an opportunity to do so.

I find the discussion in Chapter 11 very interesting, in which the different reasons for and timing of draw offers are considered. I cannot remember this subject being addressed that often before. A draw offer can have a profound psychological effect, which should not be underestimated.

Finally, in Chapter 12, I propose that we should not at the end of the day take things too seriously. At least we can learn to accept things that go wrong as part of life. Learning from these mistakes makes us stronger; in my experience these low moments can make or break you.

7 Behaviour On and Off the Board

Most of this chapter may perhaps seem like common sense, but personally speaking I have learnt at least one or two of these lessons the hard way. Moreover, on more than one occasion I have seen younger players 'brow beaten' by adults who should have known better and so I thought that a few practical tips on what to do in 'a situation' would be useful. Finally, I have included a section on how to deal with problems relating to queries on how an event is controlled.

The first point I would like to make is about people who discuss their own positions during a game. This can vary from idle, and quite innocent, 'chit-chat' to outright cheating. In its simplest form, somebody asks how you are doing, more out of politeness or curiosity than anything else. In this situation I think the simplest thing to do is just to say that "it's too early to say" or "God knows" and leave it at that, preferably then making a polite retreat or changing the subject. Some players get paranoid about others discussing their games (and in some ways quite rightly so) but should avoid letting this interfere with their concentration or the task at hand. People who do discuss positions in progress soon get a 'reputation' and become unpopular or ostracized by stronger players who know how hard it is to obtain a good reputation and how easy it is to lose it. Players who spend periods away from the board in the company of strong players or in particular with family members who are strong players need to be conscious of this and be careful not to have their actions misconstrued.

Another activity that should be carefully avoided is that of looking at a bookstall during your game. You may absentmindedly, and quite innocently, have had your attention caught by something that is totally irrelevant to your game, but I know from my youth of one very talented player who was banned for life from the British Championships for being caught at the bookstall looking at an opening book on the line he was playing at the time. The simple answer is it isn't worth it and no amount of excuse-making could save the day if you were caught.

Personal mannerisms can be annoying but most people with them are oblivious to their own behaviour. Foot-tapping, muttering, etc., should if possible just be put out of your mind, although I must admit my pet hate is people who stand behind me jangling coins! This is still a mannerism and should be differentiated from someone who, for instance, makes notes on their scoresheet; this is just wrong and, although I doubt that I would personally complain, I would almost certainly be curt with them afterwards away from the board. Another annoying thing is when a crowd gathers around a game during a tight finish, often when the players are in time-trouble and insists on being noisy, or players who finish and then, as if their game was the only one that counts for anything at all, talk excessively loudly, disturbing those who are still playing – take it outside and discuss the game to your heart's content. I know at times it's almost a case of release of tension but people need to consider others. If you are still playing and are disturbed, try to shut yourself off, but if you find it necessary, a loud "sshh!" and a filthy look normally does the trick.

If there is a problem at the board, whether you believe your opponent has behaved improperly or you have a dispute of any concern, the best thing to do is to stop the clock (and insist it remains stopped!) and call in a controller. Avoid if possible getting heated, even let your opponent have the first say (it gives you extra time to rationalize and collate your thoughts) and put across your point of view as clearly and even-temperedly as you can (the controller hasn't done anything to you – yet!). It is also vital in my mind to keep the discussion between the players and the controller; at times third parties butt in and often the key points can get confused or lost in the ensuing

talks (arguments). If somebody else is needed as an independent witness, there is a time and place for their evidence to be given. If the controller's decision seems to be wrong, consider whether you believe him to be proficient. If the answer is yes, then get on with the task at hand. If not, then ask if he could refer the matter to another controller – if possible, one you know to be competent and see what his views are. You have to be extremely careful that you do not let the matter affect your state of mind for the game, following games, the whole tournament, the rest of your life... If possible, accept it as 'one of those things' and try, especially if the game is against a player with whom you were previously on good terms, not to let it spoil a friendship; it isn't worth it.

To juniors, I would recommend that you do not let your opponent push you into accepting what he says as correct; he may be mistaken or 'trying it on'. It is doubtful that the situation can be successfully resolved after the game has finished; it may seem just a case of sour grapes. Be polite, stop the clocks and call in a controller, just to check. In junior leagues I've had players accept from their opponents that they only have twenty-five moves to win when they get down to a bare king, that they cannot win with ♔+♖ vs ♔ or that three checks in a row means that the game is a draw! It is no good crying over spilt milk afterwards. I explain that, with the best will in the world, your opponent hasn't got **your** interests at heart.

As far as controllers are concerned, my attitude has changed over the years. At one time, as a qualified British Chess Federation arbiter myself, I used to argue about anything that was obviously wrong. What I found from experience is that this invariably put me in the wrong frame of mind for my following game whether things had been properly resolved or not. If you feel something, for example a pairing, is obviously incorrect, the best thing you can do is to get the controller involved to the side at a convenient moment and ask him to explain for your benefit how the pairings arose. This takes a lot of pressure off the controller if he notices the mistake himself and allows him to save face in correcting the error himself. Moreover, if the pairings turned out to be right for some reason, you haven't put yourself in his bad books or looked stupid. It must be remembered that controlling an event is, at the best of times, a thankless task, and that when the controllers are under great pressure, especially when there are three rounds in a day or it is a quickplay event, a great deal of latitude should be given.

8 Knowing the Rules

This short chapter is designed to answer several basic questions that have arisen over the years as to the correct way of doing things.

a) Stopping the clock with the same hand as that which moves the piece is a good habit as well as a requirement. The basic idea is that this ensures that the move has been completed **prior** to the clock being stopped.

b) You can claim a draw, providing you have a complete, up-to-date, legible scoresheet, if you and your opponent have made 50 moves without a piece being taken or a pawn being moved. This is true now no matter what material is on the board. At one time 'extensions' to 75 or 100 moves were granted in various situations where more than 50 moves may be required to force a win, e.g. ♖+♗ vs ♖ or 2♘ vs ♙ when the pawn is on certain squares. I vaguely remember a game of Miles's years ago where he had been defending ♖+♗ vs ♖ for some time, eventually erred but managed to claim a draw under the fifty-move rule just before his opponent could give mate!

c) You are required to keep an up-to-date, legible scoresheet until you have less than five minutes on your clock. Note that a recent rule change has made it permissible to reply to your opponent's last move before writing either move down, but you must

have written these moves down before making your next move.

d) Once a time-control is reached, if either player has not been writing down all the moves (due to time-shortage) he must bring his scoresheet up to date during his own time (even if it is his opponent's move, his own clock should be restarted while he completes this task).

e) To reach the time-control you must make the last move and stop your clock before your flag falls. The only exception is for a legal move that gives checkmate or stalemate, as this ends the game immediately.

f) As we all know, it is possible to claim a draw if the position is repeated three times. However, in recent years, there has been some clarification of what qualifies as a repetition of position, and changes in the method of making the claim. The same position must have occurred three times at some point, **any point**, in the game with the same options, i.e. any castling or *en passant* possibilities must have been identical in all three cases. To claim a draw by threefold repetition you should write down your next move on your scoresheet (but **not** play it on the board) and tell your opponent that you are claiming the draw (if you play your move on the board, you cannot claim a draw and your opponent is entitled to continue). Then you should leave your clock running and call in the controller (unless of course your opponent accepts your claim). You cannot lose on time providing your claim is correct – on verifying your claim the controller will award the draw. Once you have made the claim, you cannot retract it.

g) Under some sets of rules, there are provisions to prevent a player trying to win a drawn position purely on the clock. It is your responsibility to check exactly what these rules are, and how to make the claim. The following is typical. In claiming that your opponent is not trying to win the game by normal means when you are short of time (2-3 minutes or less is a good guideline) stop the clock and call in the controller telling him of your claim. The controller should then ask you to continue, so that he can verify that your opponent is trying to win purely on time. He may award you the draw even if your flag falls providing he is happy that **you** have demonstrated the draw. It should be said that the emphasis is as much, if not more, on the player short of time to show that he can draw the position without real effort.

h) When castling, move the king first. The rules have changed over the years from having to make a rook move if you touch the rook first, to a warning if you touch the rook first but castle without hesitation, and so on. The easiest thing is just to get into the correct habit of moving the king first when castling.

Knowing the Rules – Exercises

The solutions are given on pages 136-7.

1) After the moves **1 e4 d6 2 d4 ♘f6 3 ♘c3 g6 4 f4 ♗g7 5 e5 dxe5 6 dxe5 ♕xd1+ 7 ♔xd1 ♘g4 8 ♔e1 f6 9 h3 ♘h6 10 exf6 exf6 11 ♗e3 c6** White attempts to castle queenside. What do you do?

2)

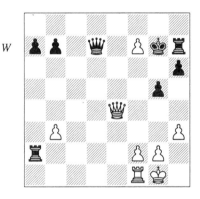

In mutual time shortage White continues **1 ♕xh7+! ♔xh7 2 f8**. However, when he promotes, he leaves the pawn on the eighth rank, restarts your clock and within seconds announces check. What do you do?

3)

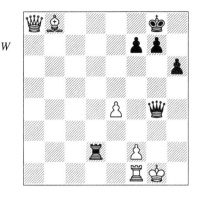

The moves leading up to the time-control were **1 ♔h2 ♕h4+ 2 ♔g2 ♕g4+ 3 ♔h2 ♕h4+ 4 ♔g1 ♕g4+ 5 ♔h2 ♕h4+**. On playing 5...♕h4+ Black claimed the draw. What do you do?

4)

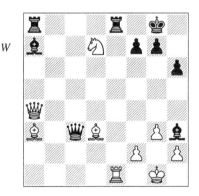

With the time-control at move forty the game concluded **37 ♖xe8+ ♖xe8 38 ♘f6+ gxf6 39 ♕xe8+ ♔g7 40 ♕f8#**. Your opponent points out that your flag has fallen, and a spectator who had been watching for some time states that it had fallen as early as move 38. What do you do?

5)

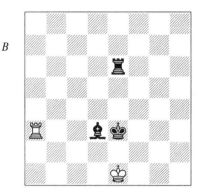

Black now plays **110...♖f6**. The last capture or pawn move was on White's 61st move.

What do you do?

6) In his time-trouble your opponent, as Black, hasn't recorded his last eight moves up to the time-control. On making his 40th move he starts your clock and confirms he has reached the number of moves required. What do you do?

9 Clock-Handling

The way in which you use the clock is an acquired skill in itself. There are two extremes of poor clock-handling. Firstly there is the failure to use your time for careful consideration, a problem especially with very young players, who almost insist on moving the 'piece nearest their hand'. At the other end are 'time-trouble freaks', who insist on leaving themselves vast numbers of moves to make in practically no time at all, even in simplified positions which are obviously good. This is asking for trouble. I think the reason why they continue with their habit, though, is that more often than not they are allowed to get away with it. I have lost count of the number of times I have seen the opponent of somebody in extreme time-trouble trying to 'match them for pace' and thus blowing any advantage or opportunity to give them practical problems.

Nunn defines time-trouble in his excellent and entertaining book *Secrets of Practical Chess* as when a player has the equivalent of a minute a move or less. He quite rightly points out that some players find it hard to cope when they get down to their last ten minutes even when they only have a handful of moves to make while others seem under no burden or pressure when they have ten or so to make in their final minute.

Here is an example of such a situation:

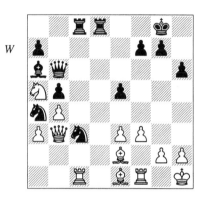

Sheldon – Panczyk
Newport 1999

Black had been exerting pressure throughout the game, but now things had got out of control. At this point White had about two or three minutes to reach the time-control at move 40 while Black had in the region of ten. I therefore expected White to fold under the pressure of her experienced International Master opponent. We will take up the game from here.

28 ♗xc3 ♛xe3 29 ♗xe5?

29 ♗c4! leaves White reasonably placed, e.g. 29...♘xc3 30 ♗xf7+ ♔h8 31 ♖ce1 and White may even be better, but there is still a lot of chess to be played.

29...♕xc1 30 h3 ♕c2?!

In Black's rush to exchange queens he misses a straightforward route to victory with 30...♕d2! 31 ♕d1 ♕e3! 32 ♕a1 ♖c2!, when White can think of resigning.

31 ♕e3 ♕d2

31...♘c3, bringing the knight back into play, seems like a natural alternative, but Black persists in his idea of attempting to exchange queens.

32 ♕e4 ♘c3

32...f5!? may well be best although with the clock ticking I can understand Black's reluctance to allow White's pieces to storm in. However, as the following variation shows, it amounts to little in reality: 33 ♕h4 ♕xe2 34 ♕e7 ♖d7! 35 ♕xd7 ♕xe5 36 ♘c6 ♕e8 37 ♘e7+ ♔h8 38 ♕e6 ♖b8 39 ♖e1 ♖b6! and White's attack runs out of steam.

33 ♕g4 ♕g5?

33...g6 is almost certainly best; after 34 ♕h4 ♖e8 35 ♕f6 ♖xe5 36 ♕xe5 ♕xe2 White has no survival chances.

34 f4!

And all of a sudden Black's advantage is not so obvious, ironically at the point where for the first time he is allowed to make the exchange of queens he was so desperate for.

34...♕g6?

Black avoids the immediate exchange, which seems inconsistent with his previous policy. 34...♕xg4! 35 ♗xg4 ♘e4 36 ♗xc8 ♘g3+ 37 ♔g1 ♖xc8 38 ♖e1 leads to an approximately level position.

35 ♕xg6 fxg6 36 ♗g4 ♖a8??

36...♘e4 is still relatively best.

37 ♗xc3 ♗c8?? 38 ♗f3 ♖b8 39 ♗e5 ♖b6 40 ♗c7 ♖d3 41 ♗xb6 axb6 42 ♘c6 1-0

And with the time-control safely reached, Black resigns. Surprisingly Black still had more time left on his clock at the point that the time-control was reached. It was noticeable during this period that White seemed relaxed and in control while Black seemed panicky and nervous. Given the starting position and clock times you may have expected this to be the other way round. I put this down to:

a) Ruth Sheldon being used to time-pressure.

b) Krzysztof Panczyk being a good positional player who has not played a lot of quality chess recently and therefore had not found his 'touch'. Also he is not a very good blitz player for a player of his standard.

We now look at a good example of how to pose problems for an opponent who is in time-pressure. It involves a very young Nigel Short (as an untitled player!) against the seasoned grandmaster Robert Byrne from *The Master Game* 1981 (*see diagram on following page*). For those who don't remember it, *The Master Game* was a series on British television in which the players recreated their thoughts during a game for the benefit of the television audience. The players' comments, as quoted here, are from *The Master Game – Book 2*, by Jeremy James and William Hartston.

White has more space but Black is very solid and has chances to prepare

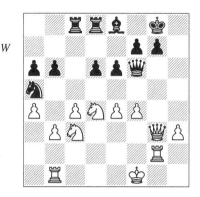

Short – R. Byrne
London (Master Game) 1981

the thematic breaks of ...b6-b5 or ...d6-d5 in his own time. However, with five moves to make to the time-control and little time to calculate, White launches a vicious attacking move which was described by Bill Hartston as "a fine blend of optimism, courage and sheer bluff".

36 ♘f5!?

Byrne: "Oh, I overlooked that. I really don't know if it's right, it may be dead wrong, but I've only a minute on my clock and I don't want to have to defend instead of attack. If I take that knight, ♘d5, ♕h6; ♘e7+, ♔f8; ♘xf5, ♕f6; ♘xg7, then he's going to try to bring the rook to the e-line to cut off my king, move the knight away and give mate with the queen on g8. What defence would I have against that? ♗d7, ♗c6, oh he would do that right in my time-pressure. What a brat! I'm afraid I wouldn't be able to handle that. I'll just have to grab something reasonably safe."

36...g6?

In fact, after 36...exf5 37 ♘d5 ♕h6 38 ♘e7+ ♔f8 39 ♘xf5 ♕h7! 40 ♘xg7 ♗c6 White has insufficient compensation for the piece.

Short: "Isn't that a blunder? I thought that he had to take the knight on f5. I've got the move ♘xd6 now, threatening his rook on c8, and if he plays ♖xd6, e5. This seems crushing."

37 ♘xd6!

Byrne: "Oh damn! If I had seen that I would have taken the knight no matter what, because this is ridiculous. One move and I'm lost, completely lost. Taking the knight of course is a fork with e5, but if I don't take the knight it's worse yet. If I save that rook, he plays e5, ♕g7; he just piles in with ♘ce4 to f6 check. It's destruction. This thing is totally gone, but at least I don't want to overstep [lose on time]. I just have to fish as best I can."

37...♖xd6 38 e5 ♕f5

Short: "Now I have a tremendous position. I better take his rook off now."

39 exd6

Byrne: "There are no rational moves here; this is awful. The only thing to do is just mess it up, therefore b5."

39...b5 40 ♖d1 ♗c6

"Byrne has reached the time control, but he is the exchange down, and White's d-pawn looks tremendous. Really the win should be a formality." (Hartston). However, with time on his clock Byrne found a way to make things tricky and owing to his youth and inexperience Short blundered his d-pawn, the game eventually ending in a draw.

The fact of the matter, though, is that Short picked a well-timed moment, in his opponent's time-pressure, to 'mix things' and that Byrne tried to be practical and play 'something safe'. Normally this would be a wise precaution, aiming to put off a difficult decision until he had more time available to evaluate the ramifications. In this instance, however, 36...g6 was not at all safe, but a clear blunder. Byrne was forced into making a panicky decision, and it is not surprising that he got it wrong with just a minute left on his clock – his concrete analysis and calculating time was spent on 36...exf5 and therefore no time was used on the tactical side of 36...g6, which was played on the basis of zero calculation.

The following example, while in some ways not as dramatic, is another example of a bad time-trouble error:

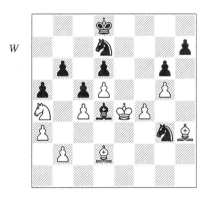

Pein – McNab
British League (4NCL) 1998/9

40 ♔d3??

The question marks are not for the move itself but for the repercussions, as soon will become clear.

40...♘f5 ½-½

Black claimed a draw by threefold repetition, as the same position had been reached twice earlier, on moves 36 and 38. With White being the shorter of time he decided to 'play it safe' to make the time-control before forming a plan to turn the screws. However, he hadn't realized 40...♘f5 was a threefold repetition. With more time he could have checked on this and then played 40 ♔f3. He could subsequently have arranged to put his king back on d3 without repeating before playing ♗e1!, when he could have every hope of gaining the full point.

My advice regarding clock-handling is quite simple and can be summarized as follows:

a) Move at your own pace but play the opening moves, as long as you are confident of them, at a reasonably fast pace. I remember George Botterill as Black against Murray Chandler taking over an hour to play 1...d6, 2...♘f6, 3...g6, 4...♗g7 and 5...0-0 against a 'normal' set-up at a time when he was an invariable Pirc player. This seemed to me ridiculous when they were playing a relatively fast time-limit of 48 moves in 105 minutes. It is no surprise that he later got very short of time and suffered the consequences.

b) Spend your valuable time once you are out of your known 'book' judging the position and forming a plan, calculating the timing of the specifics.

c) Don't waste time on absolutely forced moves. This may seem obvious, but should not be confused with making 'obvious' recaptures when in fact you miss an opportunity to play a *zwischenzug* (an intermediate move, often a check), alternative recapture or the advance of a strong passed pawn for example. Again I have seen players spending minutes on playing their only legal move and justifying this by telling me that they are looking at the further consequences. I don't see the point of this. You may as well play the move, see your opponent's reply and then study the position. After all, you are then one move closer to the logical conclusion of the situation and therefore your analysis should be made easier and more accurate.

d) Set yourself a point according to the time-control when you should take the practical decision to speed up, leaving yourself a sensible amount of time to reach the time-control. This gives you more leeway should the position become unexpectedly complex. My own view is the only time you should get into extreme time-trouble is if you are distinctly worse and need to 'invest' large amounts of time to keep the position alive, or in the hope your opponent will get over-excited and try to 'blitz' you.

e) If you get into time-trouble, be practical and try to rely on instinct rather than large amounts of calculation. Your 'gut reaction' is more likely to be correct than hurried tactical

processing when 'missing one move' can prove disastrous.

f) If your opponent is in time-trouble, and you are better or at least no worse, move at your own pace, setting him awkward practical decisions to make. If you feel you are quite a bit worse, then look for an opportunity to complicate, without going over the top. Often, as in the Short-Byrne case, you may have the choice between a sensible, quiet approach or entering complications involving a material imbalance. In particular, if you enter complications try to avoid variations where your opponent's moves are obvious or more or less forced, as it is then you who has to make the pace.

g) One practical tip if you are clearly worse and your opponent is very short of time (and, for instance, you have 7 or 8 minutes left and are therefore still required to notate move by move) is to let your own clock run down (using this time constructively, of course, to work out variations) to five minutes and then try to blitz him, stopping to think if your opponent plays anything unexpected.

Remember that if your opponent is a 'time-trouble freak', he is used to this situation, whereas you may be relatively inexperienced. Conversely, if your opponent plays very quickly throughout, investing time in key positions can pay dividends in that seeing one idea or consequence that your opponent fails to see can in effect end the game or totally change the assessment. In conclusion, try to play at **your** natural pace rather than your opponent's.

10 Swindling Your Opponent

Let us first of all define what a swindle is. If your opponent is clearly better to the point that he should be winning and you manage to turn things around by getting him to fall for 'tricks', then you have swindled him. Now I will explain why I have defined swindle. In order for you to trick your opponent there are a number of things you must do:

a) Accept that you should be losing. This takes pressure off you, as you then have nothing to lose. Moreover, as one of the following examples shows, it isn't necessary for the trap you set to be 100% sound, only that it sets your opponent practical problems. This can be especially useful if your opponent is in time-trouble and wants to avoid committing himself.

b) Make the trap or trick you set as devious as possible. It is especially useful if it appears to let your opponent do something that he very much wanted to do anyway.

c) Avoid alerting your opponent to the fact you have set a trap. Often I have seen players 'bang out' a move, but this is nothing short of stupid as your opponent will treat it with suspicion rather than regarding it as 'just another move'.

d) Avoid exchanges where possible, especially if you are material down, and remain active, even if this means shedding some further material.

Now let's look at some practical examples:

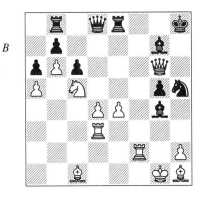

Panczyk – Baker
Hereford 1997

Here things have gone horribly wrong. I am a pawn down, my g-pawn is hanging and my major pieces are rather passively placed.

34...♖f8

Although this offers to exchange rooks, it would at least remove one of the white king's most important defenders.

35 ♗xg5

Probably technically correct, although 35 ♖xf8+ may be better on practical grounds.

35...♗xd4!?

This fails on best play but with White still having to make some 13 moves to the time-control in five minutes, it offers Black the best practical chances.

36 ♗xd8?

36 ♕h6+! ♔g8 37 ♗xd8 ♗xf2+ 38 ♔g2 is very strong for White as Black no longer has ...♘f4+ forking king and queen.

36...♗xf2+ 37 ♔f1 ♗xc5+ *(D)*

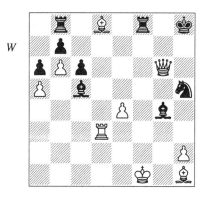

38 ♔e1??

38 ♗f3! is White's best try although after 38...♗xf3 39 ♕h6+ ♔g8 40 ♕g5+ ♘g7 41 ♗f6 ♖xf6 42 ♕xf6 ♖f8 43 ♖d8 ♗xe4 the position remains unclear. I think by this stage, though, White was a little 'punch-drunk'.

38...♗b4+ 39 ♖d2 ♖bxd8 40 ♕xg4 ♗xd2+

The tables have turned, leaving Black with a huge material advantage. In fact, though, with less than a minute to go to the time-control I managed to let things slip. The game eventually ended in a draw, although this was still enough for me to win the tournament.

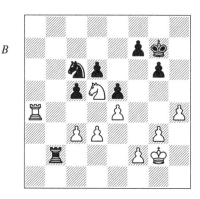

Ferguson – Baker
Hastings Challengers 1997/8

Here my position looks bleak. Not only am I a pawn down but my backward d-pawn is weak and I have no active squares for my knight.

36...♘d8!

I was determined to activate this piece even at the cost of my d-pawn.

37 ♖a6 ♘e6 38 ♖xd6 c4!

Offering the best swindling chances.

39 ♘b4

After 39 dxc4 ♘c5 40 ♘f6 (or 40 ♔f3!? ♖xf2+ 41 ♔xf2 ♘xe4+ 42 ♔f3 ♘xd6 43 c5 ♘c8 and White is still on top) 40...♖c2 41 ♖c6 ♘d3 42 ♘g4 f5 43 ♖c7+ ♔f8 44 ♖d7 ♖d2 it remains tricky for White to exploit his material advantage. However, White wants to keep 'control' of the position and to play it safe.

39...♘c5 40 ♔f3

40 ♖d5!? ♘a4 41 dxc4 ♘xc3 42 ♘d3 ♖d2 and things are still awkward.

40...♖b3 41 ♖c6 ♘xd3 42 ♘xd3 ♖xc3 43 ♔g4 ♖xd3 44 ♖xc4

Now Black has reached a technically drawn $\mathbb{I}+4\triangle$ vs $\mathbb{I}+3\triangle$ ending, which he managed to draw.

And finally...

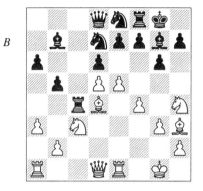

C. Morris – Baker
Cardiff 1998

I had handled the opening badly and needed to make a decision about how best to cope with the task in hand. My opponent has more space and my pieces are very congested, so I felt it was time to give up some material to gain activity.

18...②c7! 19 ②f1 dxe5 20 fxe5 ②xc3 21 bxc3 ②xd5

I would have preferred 21...②xd5 but was concerned about 22 e6.

22 ②g2 ②e6 23 a4?!

White naturally tries to undermine Black's queenside pawns but allows Black to set a devious trap.

23...b4! 24 cxb4

My opponent admitted afterwards to thinking my last move was just an act of desperation.

24...②xd4! 25 ∰xd4 ②xe5 26 ∄xe5 ②xg2! 27 ∰xd8 ∄xd8 28 ∄xe7 ②c6!

With an evil threat of ...②d4, mating! Objectively White is still doing all right and should concentrate shortly on exchanging off Black's a-pawn.

29 ∄ae1 ②d4+ 30 ∄1e3 ∄b8 31 ②xa6 ∄xb4 32 a5 ∄a4 33 ⌖f2 ∄xa5 34 ②c4 *(D)*

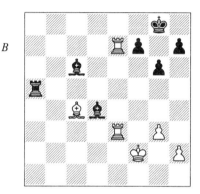

Objectively the position is still drawn – so it is time to swindle him some more!

34...②d5!

Inviting White's reply.

35 ∄e5?? ②xe3+ 36 ⌖xe3 ∄a3+ 37 ⌖d4 ②xc4 38 ⌖xc4 ∄a2!

This wins another white pawn by force.

39 h4 ∄a3 40 ∄g5 h6 41 ∄g4? ∄a4+ 0-1

It is fun to swindle your opponent but I suggest we keep things in perspective and do it as a last resort rather than continually aiming for bad positions.

11 When to Offer a Draw

It is a good idea not to offer many draws. When there is still some play left in the position, we should fight to make the most of our chances, while if we are worse, there is little point offering a draw, unless there is a suitable moment when the opponent faces an awkward decision.

Generally in a game between good players there is a 'natural' drawing conclusion if the player with the potential opportunities decides not to take a risk and play for a win, as the following two examples show:

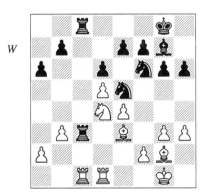

Beaumont – Baker
Newport 1999

White has an edge owing to the bishop-pair but he quickly mishandled the situation.

20 Rxc3 Rxc3 21 ⌂f1?!

Exchanging off the second pair of rooks by 21 Rc1 seems the most natural. Then the bishop-pair should offer White some practical winning chances in the ensuing ending.

21...⌂ed7 22 ⌂e2 ⌂c5!

Careful calculation shows that White is unable to trap the unprotected rook.

23 f3 ⌂fd7?

23...⌂h5! actually gives Black the advantage after 24 g4 ⌂g3+ 25 ⌂f2 ⌂e5 26 ⌂xh6.

24 ⌂d2 Rd3+ 25 ⌂e2 Rc3 26 ⌂d2 ½-½

Later in the same event, I had this position as Black:

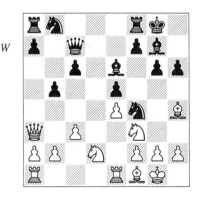

J. Cobb – Baker
Newport 1999

15 ⌂e7! Re8 16 ⌂d6 ⌂d8 17 c4!?

17 ♗xe5?? loses a piece after 17...♗xe5 18 ♘xe5 ♕xd2 19 ♖ad1 ♕c2. 17 ♕c5! may well be best.

17...a6?! 18 ♘xe5 b4! 19 ♕xb4 ♕g5 20 ♘ef3?

This is equivalent to offering a draw. To be fair, neither of us had seen the consequences of the two alternatives that would have offered White excellent chances for the full point, i.e. 20 g3! ♗xe5 21 ♘f3! (21 ♗xe5?! ♕xe5 22 gxf4 ♕xf4 leaves Black with adequate play for the pawn) 21...♗xd6 22 ♕xd6 and White remains well on top, and 20 ♘d3!, which also seems like a strong possibility.

20...♘h3+ 21 ♔h1 ♘xf2+ 22 ♔g1 ♘h3+ 23 ♔h1 ½-½

Nevertheless, I think there are times when it can be a good idea to offer a draw and conversely bad times to offer one. Let's take a look at some examples from my own games when draw offers have been made.

Black has just played 20...h6x♗g5. As I took the bishop, I offered a draw. The following considerations apply:

a) Prior to this game my score was 2½/3 against him.

b) We had both started the tournament badly/indifferently and so a steady draw would do neither of us much harm.

c) I wasn't giving much away, as White has an edge and, if he so wished, could easily exchange both pairs of rooks on the d-file, leading to a very level opposite-coloured bishop ending. This also meant that if he were to refuse, he might feel 'morally obliged' to play some enterprising/double-edged chess, offering me some practical chances as well.

In the end result, factor 'c' very much played its part. He refused the draw, sacrificed a couple of pawns for unclear but realistic attacking chances and went wrong in time-trouble, eventually losing.

Panczyk – Baker
Newport 1999

Baker – Summerscale
Hastings Challengers 1997/8

This was the final position of the game. I had just played 26 ♔g1-g2 having rejected 26 ♖a6 ♖c7 27 b4 ♔e6 28 b5 ♔d5 29 bxc6 ♔c5 with the idea of ...♔b5 as being nothing special. In the final position I feel as though White should be better on the grounds that Black's queenside pawn majority is currently irrelevant and White has a healthy passed pawn and the opportunity to create two connected passed pawns at some stage. However, a plan is not obvious and Aaron's draw offer was well timed, the basis being:

a) He offered the draw before the position could deteriorate to the point where I was obviously better or could carry on for the win without risk.

b) He knew that for me to prove anything concrete would require a lot of hard work and accurate calculation, with the risk that if I should miss something crucial in my time-trouble, the position could easily turn sour.

In the following position, we had just exchanged queens on e7 and with 20...♔f8x♕e7 Black offered a draw. I now considered the following:

a) By winning I could still finish on a plus score after a particularly 'average' tournament.

b) I had had five Blacks and four Whites and didn't want to 'waste' one of my precious Whites.

c) I had in the past got three draws as Black against this opponent, but in

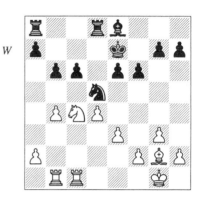

Baker – Devereaux
Newport 1999

all three had uncomfortable positions and never really had any realistic prospects for an advantage and so wanted to 'punish' him when I had a White.

d) I felt in the position in question I had an edge and could carry on relatively safely and should I pick the wrong plan it was likely that Black would get nothing more than an equal position.

Because of these factors I carried on and duly won the game (see Chapter 3, Endgame Technique). Due to all of the above I feel this was a badly-timed draw offer. It would have been better not to make the offer at all but perhaps wait until there was a more relevant moment – for example if I had mishandled the position slightly or got to a position where I had to commit myself if I wanted to go all out for the win.

12 Don't Worry – It Might Never Happen!

I could have called this chapter 'never give up' or 'try, try, try again'. The main theme game I have picked is between Grandmasters David Norwood and John Emms. After some weak opening play by White, which was energetically met by Black, most players would have fallen apart. What impressed me was the way Norwood carried on fighting almost as though nothing had happened and it was 'business as usual'. It just goes to show how hard it is to put a grandmaster away!

Norwood – Emms
British League (4NCL) 1998/9

1 g3 c5 2 c4 g6 3 d4?!

It is not a great idea to bring the queen out too early – ask any beginner! Seriously though, sooner or later Black will gain a useful tempo with ...♘c6.

3...cxd4 4 ♕xd4 ♘f6 5 ♘c3 ♗g7 6 ♗g2 ♘c6 7 ♕d2 0-0 8 ♘h3 ♘a5 9 ♕d3

The odd-looking 9 c5 may well be best, while 9 b3 is nicely met by 9...d5, e.g. 10 cxd5 ♘xd5 11 ♘xd5 (after 11 ♗xd5!? ♗xc3 12 ♕xc3 ♕xd5 13 ♖g1! ♗xh3 14 ♗h6 f6 15 g4 ♖fd8 16 ♕xh3 Black's position seems the more

comfortable) 11...♗xa1, when White's compensation for the exchange seems inadequate.

9...♕c7 10 b3 d5! 11 cxd5 ♗f5 12 ♕d2 ♘e4!

Black's energetic play springs from his more harmonious development and castled king. White is in trouble.

13 ♘xe4 ♗xe4 (D)

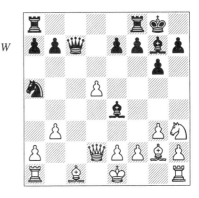

Now, with ...♗xa1, ...♗xg2 and ...♗c3 threatened, a lot of players as White would resign. Norwood instead makes the correct practical decision to shed material in order to remain relatively solid, active and at last get some sort of coordination into his position.

14 ♗xe4 ♗c3 15 ♗b2 ♗xd2+ 16 ♔xd2 ♕b6 17 ♗c3 ♖ac8 18 ♖ac1 ♖fd8 19 ♘f4 ♘c6 20 ♘d3

Finally, White seems to have some sort of position; now the only real problem is his material deficiency. The fact that material is 'imbalanced' rather than White just being material down makes it more difficult for Black to realize his advantage.

20...♘d4 21 ♗g2 ♖xc3

Black returns a small amount of material to try to break through and remove both White's bishop-pair and his control of the dark squares. It does, however, leave White closer to material equality.

22 ♖xc3 ♕a5!

Winning the a-pawn.

23 ♖c1 ♕xa2+ 24 ♔e3 (D)

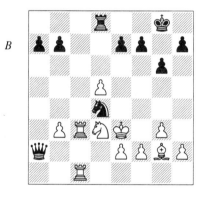

24...♘xe2?!

After 24...e5, 25 ♘xe5? loses to 25...♕xe2+ 26 ♔xd4 ♕xf2+, so White would have had to try 25 ♗f3 or 25 ♗f1, but neither seems overly attractive.

25 ♖c8 ♖xc8 26 ♖xc8+ ♔g7 27 ♖c7 ♘g1 28 ♖xb7 a5

After 28...♕e2+!? 29 ♔d4 ♕d2 30 ♖xe7 ♘e2+ 31 ♖xe2 ♕xe2 32 b4

Black still has work to do to realize his material advantage.

29 ♗e4 f5 30 ♗f3 ♘xf3 31 ♔xf3 ♕a3 32 ♔e3 ♔f6 33 ♖b6+ ♔g7 34 ♖b7 ♔f6 35 ♖b6+ ♔f7 36 ♔d4 ♕a1+ 37 ♔c4 a4 38 ♖a6!?

This seems suicidal as it gives Black a strong passed pawn. On the other hand, it does tie down Black's queen, at least temporarily.

38...a3 39 ♖a7 a2

39...♔f6 may be better as after 40 ♖a6+ Black can play 40...♔g7, cutting down White's counterplay.

40 d6 ♔e8?

40...♕b1! 41 d7 ♕c2+ 42 ♔d4 e5+! 43 ♘xe5+ ♔e7 and Black wins.

41 d7+ ♔d8 42 ♘c5 ♕f1+ 43 ♔d5 ♕d1+ 44 ♔c6 ♕d6+ 45 ♔b5 ♕b8+ 46 ♔c6 ♕d6+ ½-½

The next example (*see diagram on following page*) illustrates several points I have stressed in this book. It also illustrates an approach to positions that I encourage readers to adopt if they wish to win more games: if you don't think you should lose the position, then there is every justification to play it on for a win!

42 h4??

This would also be a good example of how *not* to play in time-trouble. On the last move before the time-control, White commits himself with 42 h4. Instead, I could have played one non-committal move, and then timed the h4 advance at my leisure after removing my king from g3. Then after ...gxh4, the move ♕f4 would have forced capitulation.

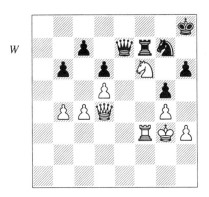

Baker – Franklin
Torquay 1998

42...gxh4+ 43 ♔f2 ♕e5

At this point Black is objectively fine and only the 'will to win' combined with the eye of a swindler carried the day in the end.

44 ♕xe5 dxe5 45 c5 bxc5 46 bxc5 h3 47 g5! ♘e8!

47...hxg5 48 ♖xh3+ ♘h5 49 ♖xh5+ ♔g7 50 ♖xg5+ ♔xf6 51 ♖g8 gives White the better practical chances, although the position should still be drawn with best play.

48 ♖xh3

After 48 ♘xe8 h2 49 ♖xf7 h1♕ 50 g6 Black has to take the perpetual as 50...♕h2+ 51 ♔e3 ♕g3+ 52 ♔e2 ♕xg6?? 53 ♖f8+ ♔h7 54 ♘f6+ ♔g7 55 ♖g8+ ♔xf6 56 ♖xg6+ ♔xg6 57 d6 enables White to win the ♔+♙ ending.

48...♘xf6 49 gxf6

49 ♖xh6+ ♘h7+ unfortunately is check; otherwise 50 g6 would be strong.

49...♖xf6+ 50 ♔e3 ♔g7 51 ♔e4 ♔f7 52 ♔xe5 ♔e7?!

52...♖g6 would have been better.

53 ♖g3 ♖f7 54 ♖g8 ♖h7??

54...♖f1 might still have saved the day.

55 c6! 1-0

Black resigned due to 55...♔f7 56 ♖d8 ♔g6 57 d6 cxd6+ 58 ♔xd6 h5 59 c7 ♖xc7 60 ♔xc7, when Black's ♔+♙ are not far enough advanced to cause problems.

Another comforting thought at the board is that when an opponent plays the opening and the middlegame well, then maybe his endings are poor! Possibly this is just over-optimism but time and time again it has proved to be the case. The following example shows that one mustn't take too many liberties in this respect though.

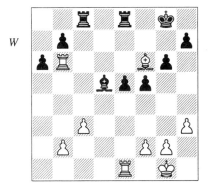

Baker – A. Webster
Cardiff 1998

After being under some pressure I had at last reached a reasonable position. I now made the fatal mistake of prematurely relaxing.

29 ♖xe5?

After 29 ♖d6! White should have no great problems. Instead, I 'preferred' to make the rook on b6 as inactive as possible.

29...♗c6 30 f4 ♔f7 31 ♖xe8 ♖xe8 32 ♗e5 g5

With time-trouble, looming further inaccuracies from me were not far behind.

33 g3?!

33 ♔f2 may well have been best. It has the merit of stopping Black's rook from penetrating to the seventh rank.

33...gxf4 34 ♗xf4 ♖e2 35 ♖b4

Hoping to activate the rook.

35...a5 36 ♖b6 ♖g2+ 37 ♔f1 ♖h2 38 h4 ♔g6 39 b4?!

To be honest this was based on a miscalculation.

39...a4 40 b5 ♖b2 41 c4

41 ♗c1! ♖xb5 42 ♖xb5 ♗xb5+ 43 ♔f2 gives White some chances of holding the position, although it would have been a thankless task.

41...a3! 42 ♗e5 ♖b1+ 43 ♔e2 ♔h5 44 ♖xc6 bxc6 45 bxc6 ♖b6! 46 c7 ♖c6

White is totally lost.

Not to be outdone, the following diagram is an example of mine where the boot was on the other foot.

White has some 'optical' pressure against e6 and so will get his rook to the only open file more quickly. However, Black is solid and has the better pawn-structure. Once he has relieved pressure on the a2-g8 diagonal, he can expect at least equality. Moreover, the presence of opposite-coloured bishops

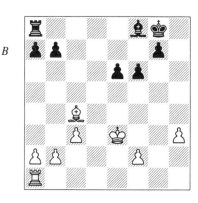

Baker – J. Richards
Bristol Ch 1997

tends to make things drawish, especially if the rooks were to be exchanged.

32...♔f7 33 ♖d1 ♔e7

33...♗c5+ seems a natural alternative although unpinning the e-pawn looks very sensible.

34 f4 ♖c8

34...g5!, exchanging off another pawn while creating a passed pawn of his own, would seem reasonable.

35 ♗b3 b5 36 ♖d4 ♖c5 37 ♖e4 e5 38 f5!

This ties down Black's kingside as well as increasing the scope of the bishop on the a2-g8 diagonal.

38...♖c6 39 a4!

It is now time for White to utilize his queenside majority and also to penetrate with his rook on the queenside if possible.

39...♖b6 40 ♗g8 bxa4 41 ♖xa4 ♖xb2 42 ♖xa7+ ♔d8

42...♔d6 43 ♖f7 ♖b8 44 ♔e4 ♖c8 45 h4 leaves White with some sort of an edge, although a lot of work still needs to be done. However, 42...♔d6 seems more natural than the text-move.

43 ♔e4 ♖c2?!

This loses a tempo over the immediate 43...♖h2.

44 c4 ♖h2 45 ♖a8+ ♔e7 46 c5 ♖xh3 47 c6

'Charlie the c-pawn' is on the move!

47...♔d6

At the time, I felt this was a step in the wrong direction. However, after 47...♖c3 48 ♔d5 ♖d3+ 49 ♔c5 ♖d8 50 ♖a7+ ♔e8+ 51 ♔c4 ♖d4+ 52 ♔b5 Black has serious problems.

48 ♖xf8 ♔xc6 49 ♖f7?!

49 ♗e6 would be a better try.

49...♖g3??

Now White mops up. 49...♖h4+ would have drawn, as White cannot evade the checks without losing his last pawn.

50 ♗h7 ♖g4+ 51 ♔f3 ♖b4 52 ♖xg7 ♖b7 53 ♖xb7 ♔xb7 54 ♗g8 ♔c6 55 ♔e4 1-0

The main thing I wanted this section to illustrate was how the 'will to win' (or at least survive!) coupled with the need to remain vigilant even in positions which a lot of people would just dismiss as 'an obvious draw' are two attributes of the fighting player.

Part 3: After the Game

After a game it is important to take stock of what went right and what went wrong, and to make any necessary adjustments in our approach or repertoire. However, all too often, whether due to laziness or the inability to face the facts, we fail to do so. The upshot is that we fail to learn our lesson, and are doomed to repeat the same mistakes. You owe it to yourself to play through your games and have them available for future reference; this is the first means of self-help. Once in a while you should take a detailed look at your overall results and identify any major areas where you are falling down, and perhaps find some aspects of the game in which you are successful. This will help you to see what types of positions to aim for, and the areas of your game you need to work on. I provide further details and examples in Chapter 13.

After a bad game or a disappointing result, it is easy to feel despondent, especially if we lost after the opponent played a tactic which was in fact faulty. Another thing that can affect you mentally throughout the remainder of the tournament at hand is if you suffer a loss due to your opponent playing something that comes as a 'bolt from the blue'. You need to accept that in that instance he saw something that you didn't, and to realize that it is more than possible that you saw things that he didn't and it's just that they didn't become relevant or actually happen in the game, which was just a trick of fate. We look at faulty tactics and bolts from the blue in Chapters 14 and 16 respectively.

Nowadays there are undoubtedly some excellent articles and reference works on computer aids within chess but I generally find that although they may be technically excellent, that they go a little above my head and therefore they lose me and the information just doesn't register. In Chapter 17, I have tried to put across a clear guide on what a compute system can do for you, to help you get as much practical benefit as possible. On that note I should say that one of the problems is that the specification and the capabilities of systems you can buy seem to change almost by the day. With prices also coming down, the temptation is to wait for the 'perfect' computer system, with the result that you never actually obtain the system that you need. In the final analysis, if you can get and afford the system that will do what you need, then the changes that come about are almost irrelevant. After all, if something then comes along onto the market that 'your life would not be complete without', I'm sure you would find a way to justify yourself upgrading or changing your system. We must, after all, get our priorities right!

13 Analysing Your Results

If you were asked how you performed with your openings as White or Black over the last two years (or over, for instance, your last 100 games, whichever is the sooner) how would you answer? Would you be honest or go on the defensive? Would you honestly know? The easiest way would be to make a list of your results by colour and opening from your records (you see, they do come in handy sometimes) and work out the percentages you scored and your grading performance. Let us look at two mythical examples.

The first is **George** who plays in the first division of his local league,

generally on board three or four. George also plays in a limited number of weekend tournaments in either the Major or Open, depending on how he feels and the grading limits for the events. George has a BCF (British Chess Federation) grading of 155 (Elo equivalent of 1840). The two tables below give the breakdown for George.

When looking through these results and being self-critical, in a constructive manner of course, the following further points became clear:

1) After some poor results against the Pirc/Modern, George put in some hours preparing a new variation to play as White and has since scored 2/2

George (White):

Number of games	Opening	Score	Grading performance (BCF / Elo)
6	French	4½	167 / 1936
6	Pirc/Modern	2	123 / 1584
7	Caro Kann	5½	178 / 2024
23	Sicilian	13	136 / 1688

George (Black):

Number of games	Opening	Score	Grading performance (BCF / Elo)
24	Scandinavian	12½	148 / 1784
18	Dutch	10½	154 / 1832
5	Others	½	110 / 1480

and therefore nothing else needs to be done in this area at the present time.

2) George didn't like to accept the fact that his favourite line against the Sicilian, 1 e4 c5 2 c4, just didn't produce the goods. His excuse was that he hadn't the time to learn the Sicilian (in other words, Open Sicilian lines) properly due to the vast amounts of theory.

3) George felt happy on the white side of a Lopez and put his results down to a couple of blunders that had nothing to do with the opening positions he had obtained.

4) As Black he felt comfortable with the Dutch and had recently bought a good book on the Scandinavian, which he intended to use to work on a particular line against which he was experiencing problems.

5) George coped well by using his considerable experience if his opponent played 'unusual' opening systems.

Looking at these observations there were certain conclusions I reached, namely:

a) George needed to find something that was conducive with his style against the Sicilian but which didn't require an unreasonable workload to adopt.

b) He should work on the Scandinavian variations that gave him difficulties – he had already made the first step in the right direction.

c) His 'others' as Black were from the move-order 1 d4 e6 2 e4 where George had played the Owen's Defence (2...b6) and got bad positions.

Suggested course of action on top of 'b':

a) George should look through some games, preferably between strong players, in the main lines of Closed Sicilians to see if the type of positions that arose 'took his fancy'. If they didn't, then he should review other options, e.g. the 2 c3 Sicilian.

b) George told me that as Black he aimed for the Dutch by meeting 1 d4 with 1...e6 (intending 2...f5), rather than by the direct 1 d4 f5. This is because, as a younger player, he hadn't liked playing against the Staunton Gambit (1 d4 f5 2 e4). However, if White met 1...e6 with 2 e4, then this took George outside his repertoire and into positions where he scored poorly (this constituted his half out of five as Black in 'others'). I suggested that he should look through one or two recent games (again involving good players if possible) to see if he still felt the same way about the Staunton Gambit, which is nowadays viewed as rather harmless.

Our second 'survey' involves **Peter**, a 14-year-old junior with a BCF grading of 129 (Elo equivalent of 1632). Peter is very keen, and plays as much chess as he can in his local league, weekend tournaments (where he prefers playing in Majors to junior events) and some national junior events. The two tables on the following page give the breakdown for George.

Looking through the results analytically, it became immediately obvious that as White he coped very well in sharp lines in which he was well pre-pared, but not so well in 'quiet' open-ings such as the Caro-Kann and the French. Against these he played the Advance and Exchange variations re-spectively. As Black he again dealt with sharp positions very well and was up to date with the latest trends and was well prepared.

His results were less impressive when his opponent played anti-King's Indian or anti-Sicilian lines. Peter made the following admissions:

1) Against anti-Sicilians he had adopted lines suggested by friends he had spoken to at tournaments.

2) Against anti-King's Indians he had made things up as he went.

Suggested course of action:

a) Buy a good book on anti-King's Indians and anti-Sicilians.

b) Look at playing something sharper against the Caro-Kann and the French, e.g. against the Caro the main lines with 3 ♘c3, intending to meet 3...dxe4 4 ♘xe4 ♘d7 with 5 ♘g5, and against the French, to play 3 ♘c3 ready to take on the Winawer. The best way of doing this would be to look through some examples of actual play between strong players in the crucial lines. In this case Peter had Fritz 5 and access to the Internet and so could download various databases, includ-ing games from 'The Week In Chess'.

c) Try to get a strong player to look through his findings and help him get a feel for the resulting positions, play-ing some training games if possible and analysing the openings together afterwards.

d) Once he had made his choices, to stick with them for a period (rather

Peter (White):

Number of games	Opening	Score	Grading performance (BCF / Elo)
4	French	1	103 / 1424
10	Pirc/Modern	8½	155 / 1840
3	Caro-Kann	½	107 / 1456
26	Sicilian	17½	152 / 1816
4	Italian Game	3	161 / 1888

Peter (Black):

Number of games	Opening	Score	Grading performance (BCF / Elo)
22	Najdorf Sicilian	14½	162 / 1896
6	Others (e-pawn)	1½	106 / 1448
17	King's Indian	12½	157 / 1856
6	Others (d-pawn)	2	118 / 1544

than chop and change) with the view to re-analysing his results in those particular openings after a suitable period.

These are two fictitious examples and the points they raised were 'emphasized' to some extent, but I can assure you that if you go through the exercise yourself and look at things honestly and constructively that the rewards you can reap are enormous. I should know as I am convinced that this was one of the major factors in developing my own game.

14 Faulty Tactics

Just as it is vital to be constantly alert to the possibilities of putting the final touch to a game with a tactic, it is equally vital to pick holes in tactics that your opponents try or may be considering. One of the easiest ways to win a game is to 'let' your opponent play a tactic that doesn't work ... I think of this as 'the easiest way to take a piggy to market is to drag him by the tail in the opposite direction'. Here are some examples:

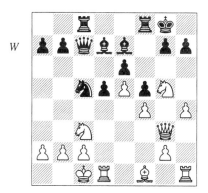

Kenworthy – Baker
British League (4NCL) 1998/9

To be fair, I hadn't really considered White's next move too seriously and therefore could be considered lucky that it wasn't stronger than it was in reality. I think my opponent played the sacrifice speculatively, on

the grounds that he didn't like his position anyway, and wanted a messy position that suited to his style, while putting me in a defensive position that would not be to my liking.

15 ♖xd5?! ♘e4!

15...exd5 16 ♘xd5 ♕d8 17 ♗c4 ♔h8 18 ♖d1 is perfectly fine for Black but I was concerned that I might miss something in this position or have problems recoordinating my pieces – White's activity may offer him some practical chances. 15...♘b3+!? 16 axb3 exd5 is another sensible option but again not totally convincing.

16 ♖xd7?!

Missing a key feature of the resulting position. However, after 16 ♘gxe4 exd5 17 ♘f6+ ♗xf6 (17...♖xf6!? 18 exf6 ♗xf6 is also very promising; Black has returned the material but has the bishop-pair and the better development, together with attacking chances along the c-file) 18 exf6 ♖xf6 Black is a fairly 'safe' exchange ahead.

16...♘xg3 17 ♖xc7 ♖xc7

Now the fact that a future ♖g1 can be met by ...♗c5 decides the issue.

18 ♘b5

18 ♘xe6 ♖xc3! 19 bxc3 ♘xh1 20 ♘xf8 ♔xf8 leaves White with insufficient compensation for the piece.

18...♗xg5 19 hxg5 ♖c5 0-1

20 ♖g1 ♘xf1 21 ♘d4 ♘g3 is hopeless as 22 ♘xe6 is met by 22...♘e2+.

B

Baker – Panczyk
Paignton Premier 1997

I had just played 18 c3!?.

18...dxc3?

It is unlucky that this enterprising sacrifice has a major flaw in it. Having said that, it is now vital for White to sort through the complications to come up with the right response.

The alternative is 18...♘c2!? 19 ♖c1 d3 20 ♖d1, when it is not clear if the passed d3-pawn is weak or strong.

19 ♖xb4!

After 19 bxc3?! ♘d3 Black's superior pawn-structure offers him some long-term advantage.

19...c2 20 ♘d4!

20 ♖e4?? loses to 20...♖d1+ 21 ♖e1 ♖xa1 22 ♖xa1 ♖d8. However, 20 ♖e1!? ♖d1 21 ♖c4 ♖e8 22 ♖f1! ♖e2 is not so clear and may well be fine for White. However, it would have led to the kind of position that would have been difficult for me to judge and left opportunities for me to get it wrong. The text-move clarifies things nicely in my favour.

20...a5!?

Too late, Black saw that 20...c5 21 ♖c4 ♖xd4 22 ♖xc5+ ♔b8 23 ♖xc2, leaves White a safe pawn ahead with good practical chances. Moreover, it is the kind of position in which Black has a thankless task.

21 ♖c4 b5 22 ♖xc2 ♖xd4 23 ♖ac1! ♖d7 24 ♖c5 ♖e8 25 ♔f1!

Stopping an immediate penetration of the black rooks to the seventh rank and leaving White well in control.

Our next example shows how missing one idea that is relevant to the 'main line' of your analysis can end in total disaster, or, as in this case, just totally throw you off your balance.

Barth – Varley
Hastings Challengers 1998/9

1 c4 ♘f6 2 ♘c3 d5 3 cxd5 ♘xd5 4 ♘f3 ♘xc3 5 bxc3 g6 6 e4 ♗g7 7 d4 c5

By transposition we have reached a normal main line in the Grünfeld.

8 ♗e2?!

This is certainly less enterprising or testing than the more normal 8 ♖b1.

8...cxd4 9 cxd4 ♘c6 10 ♗e3 ♗g4 11 d5 ♘e5 12 ♘xe5 ♗xe2 13 ♕a4+?

This is just careless and shows the value of the habit of checking routinely all of your opponent's checks, captures and ways of parrying a check. 13 ♕xe2 would leave White with a reasonable position after 13...♗xe5.

13...b5! 0-1?

The resignation seems even more incredible because after 14 ♕d4! ♗c4

(14...♕c7 15 f4 is nothing special for Black) 15 a4 (or 15 f4) White's position may be poor but it is by no means hopeless.

Our next offering is an example of how the stronger player will 'see through' superficial analysis. It is true that the combination 'merely' wins a pawn, but to a quality player this is just the thin end of the wedge.

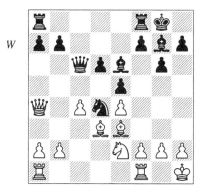

Allicock – M. Turner
British League (4NCL) 1998/9

Black has just played 14...♕b6-c6, against which White should exchange queens and realize he has little, if any, opening advantage. Having said that, his position is solid and there is a lot of chess still to be played. Instead he tried to be clever:

15 ♕d1?! ♗xc4!?

Typical of Matthew Turner – he will take any opportunity to 'mix it'.

16 ♖c1?

White carries on with his 'winning pin'. Instead after 16 ♗xd4! ♗xd3 17

♕xd3 exd4 18 ♘xd4 ♕b6 19 ♘b5! White emerges with a reasonable position.

16...♗xd3! 17 ♕xd3

Too late, White realizes that 17 ♖xc6? ♗xe2 leaves Black with far too much material for the queen.

17...♕b5! 18 ♕xb5 ♘xb5

Black is a pawn up. At this stage, White should attempt to gain some positional compensation based on the backward d-pawn and weak d5-square, e.g. 19 ♖fd1 ♖fc8 20 ♔g1, when Black still has a lot of work to do to convert his advantage into victory.

19 ♖c4 ♖fc8 20 ♖fc1 ♖xc4 21 ♖xc4 ♘d4 22 ♘xd4?

This move is based on another miscalculation, and just gives Black what he wants, by providing him with a passed pawn and bringing to life his dark-squared bishop. 22 ♘c3! is better, when with his control of the c-file and d5 available for his knight, White still has chances of play for the pawn.

22...exd4 23 ♗xd4?? b5 0-1

Black wins further material.

Finally we consider a situation that I am sure has happened to most players – you play a normal-looking tactic, and it works as planned, but at the end there is a 'sting in the tail' which turns the game in the opponent's favour. This can be put down to bad luck – your adversary hadn't a choice until the combination ended and then there it was, staring him in the face. On the other hand, maybe he seen just that little bit further – and was merely setting you up for the fall?

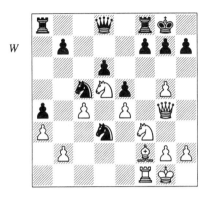

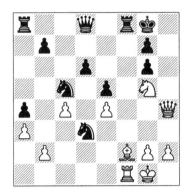

Kaufman – Tate
Fredericksburg 1999

Black had just played 20...♘b3-c5, when White produced...

21 ♘f6+!?

It is perhaps a little difficult to criticize this move too much as without it White would have little to show for his material deficit.

21...♔h8

21...gxf6?? allows 22 gxf6+ ♔h8 23 ♕g7#.

22 ♘xh7

Consistent with the previous move and very tempting in conjunction with White's 23rd.

22...♔xh7 23 g6+ fxg6 24 ♘g5+ ♔g8 25 ♕h4 *(D)*

All as planned when White played 21 ♘f6+ but now it goes horribly wrong.

25...♕xg5!?

Black heads for a clear-cut solution. 25...♖f4! is in fact good enough though: 26 ♕h7+ ♔f8 27 ♕h8+ ♔e7 28 ♕xg7+ ♔e8 and White has insufficient play for the rook.

26 ♕xg5!? ♖xf2 27 ♖xf2 ♘xf2 *(D)*

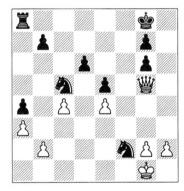

Now all becomes clear: after 28 ♔xf2, Black wins the white queen by 28...♘e4+. However, despite Black's material advantage he must be careful to keep his pieces coordinated as often a rook and two knights don't combine awfully well.

28 ♕xg6 ♘fxe4 29 g4 ♖f8 30 g5!

White has stopped any immediate back-rank mates, and gained control of the f6-square at the cost of some holes in his kingside.

30...♘d2!

Giving up the d-pawn to activate the c5-knight. 30...♖f2 leads nowhere after 31 ♕e8+ ♔h7 32 ♕h5+.

31 ♕xd6 ♖f1+ 32 ♔g2 ♖f2+!

Once again exploiting the possibility of a knight fork.

33 ♔h3 ♘ce4 34 ♕e6+?!

34 ♕xe5! seems like a better practical chance as Black must then play accurately to prove his advantage, viz. 34...♘xg5+! 35 ♔g4 (35 ♕xg5 ♖xh2+! wins the queen) 35...♖g2+ 36 ♔f5 g6+! 37 ♔f6 (37 ♔f4? ♘h3+! 38 ♔e3 ♘xc4+) 37...♘de4+ 38 ♔e7 ♖f2 39 h4 ♖f7+ and now:

a) 40 ♔e8 ♘f6+ 41 ♔d8 ♘f3 42 ♕g3 ♔g7! 43 ♔c8 ♘e4 44 ♕g4 ♘d6+ 45 ♔b8 (45 ♔d8? ♘e5 ends the game) 45...♘e5 46 ♕d4! ♘dxc4.

b) 40 ♔d8 ♖f5! 41 ♕h2 ♘f7+ 42 ♔c7 ♘fd6 and White has to sit and wait.

34...♔h7 35 g6+ ♔h6 36 ♕xe5

By playing g6+ and forcing ...♔h6 White has improved the position of the black king and made his own more vulnerable.

36...♘f3!

Once again using the recurrent theme of a knight fork.

37 ♕b8

Not 37 ♕a5? losing on the spot to 37...♘fg5+ 38 ♔g4 ♖f3.

37...♘fg5+ 38 ♔g4 ♘f6+ 39 ♔g3 ♖f3+

39...♘ge4+ is more accurate.

40 ♔g2 ♘fe4 41 h4

41 ♕h8+ ♔xg6 42 ♕e8+ ♔f5 43 ♕f8+ ♔g4 44 ♕c8+ ♔f4 45 ♕c7+ ♔e3 46 ♕b6+ ♔e2 and White finally runs out of checks, having 'forced'

Black's king to the best spot to form a mating attack.

41...♖f2+ 42 ♔h1 ♘f3!

White needs a perpetual, which sadly is lacking.

43 ♕h8+ ♔xg6 44 ♕e8+

44 h5+ ♔f7 only speeds up the process.

44...♔f5 45 ♕d7+

45 ♕f8+ ♔g4 46 ♕xg7+ ♘eg5! 47 ♕d7+ ♔xh4 is the end.

45...♔f4 46 ♕c7+ ♔e3 47 ♕b6+ ♔e2 0-1

White can no longer prevent the inevitable.

Maybe it was harsh to call White's combination 'faulty' but the fact was it just didn't work.

I hope you have found this section as interesting to play through as I did when constructing it. We have seen good players playing incorrectly, and I hope the reader draws from this the comforting conclusion that 'mere mortals' really do have a chance!

Faulty Tactics – Exercises

In the following positions there are some tactical possibilities looming. You must decide which are correct and which have 'flaws' in them. Solutions are given on pages 137-8.

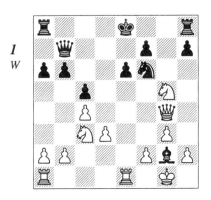

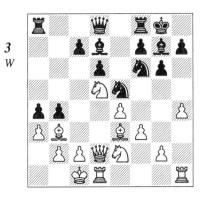

Is it correct for White to sacrifice on e6? And if so, is it necessary?

Should White exchange knights on f6 with the idea of meeting ...♕xf6 with ♗g5 and ...♗xf6 with ♗d5?

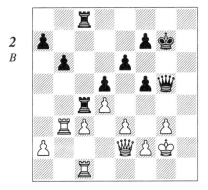

Can Black exploit the unprotected rook on c1?

How should Black cope with the menacing threats imposed by White's pawn on g6?

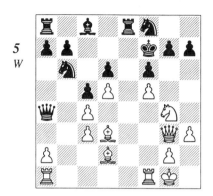

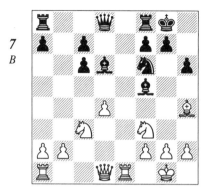

Should White sacrifice material to open up the black king?

Should Black exchange off one of his doubled c-pawns with ...c5?

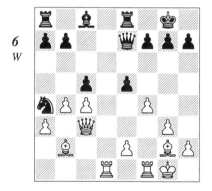

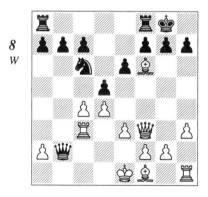

Can White afford to take on e5, threatening mate on g7?

Has White anything better than the sensible and obvious 13 ♖b3?

15 The Power of the Pieces

In this short section I will show how 'every piece has its day'. In each of the following examples we can see how the queen can, in certain specific circumstances, be 'inferior' to one of the other pieces.

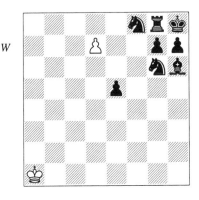

White to play and win

1 d8♘! and Black cannot avoid mate on f7. After 1 d8♕? Black would undoubtedly realize his material advantage.

F. Saavedra
Glasgow Weekly Citizen, 1895
White to play and win

1 c7 ♖d6+ 2 ♔b5 (2 ♔b7? ♖d7 draws, as does 2 ♔c5? ♖d1, when White cannot stop Black giving up the rook for the c-pawn) **2...♖d5+ 3 ♔b4 ♖d4+ 4 ♔b3** (4 ♔c3 ♖d1 5 ♔c2 transposes to the main line) **4...♖d3+ 5 ♔c2 ♖d4! 6 c8♖!!** (not 6 c8♕? ♖c4+! and after 7 ♕xc4 Black is stalemated) **6...♖a4 7 ♔b3** wins, as Black cannot both save his rook and stop mate by ♖c1#.

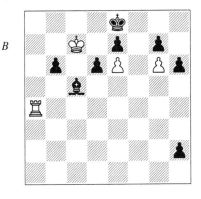

Black to play and win

After 1...h1♕ White can draw with 2 ♖a8+ ♕xa8 stalemate. However, by playing **1...h1♗!** Black should win without much trouble.

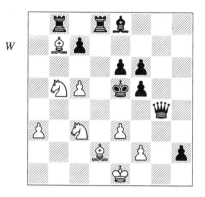

W

White to play and win

In the diagram to the left, it is not difficult to find 1 f4+ ♕xf4 2 exf4#. Had the queen on g4 been a pawn, though, White would be lost (as 1 f4+ is answered by the *en passant* capture 1...gxf3).

These all go to show something I spend a lot of time showing people I coach: although it is good to know the general value of the pieces, at the end of the day a piece is worth what the piece can do or may be able to do.

16 Bolts from the Blue

From time to time the thing I find most exciting in chess is when I watch a game and make some sort of 'spot judgement' only to see a move played that I hadn't even considered. These proverbial 'bolts from the blue' can often change the general assessment of the position and leave people in awe of the sheer imagination and depth of some players' analysis and tactical sight.

These are some of the specimens I have recently come across:

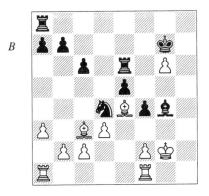

Velimirović – Skembris
Bar 1997

White had just played 25 ♗d2-c3?? (25 f3 is better, when Black only has an edge after 25...♗h5). However, he could hardly have expected...

25...♗f3+! 0-1

White resigned due to 26 ♗xf3 (26 ♔g1 ♘e2+ 27 ♔h2 ♖h8#) 26...♖xg6+ 27 ♗g4 ♖xg4+ 28 ♔h3 ♖g6!, when he is unable to stop mate.

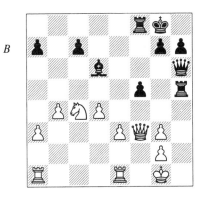

Kramnik – Bareev
Kazan ECC 1997

White had just played 24 ♕e2x♙f3, leaving him a pawn ahead in return for, one might imagine, 'some play'. He could hardly have expected...

24...♗xg3!! 25 ♕xg3 f4 26 ♕g4!

After 26 exf4 ♖xf4 27 ♖e8+ ♔f7 28 ♕xf4+ ♕xf4 Black will soon realize his material advantage.

26...fxe3 27 ♕xh5 ♕xh5 28 ♘xe3

The rest is just technique.

In the following diagram, Black has just played 26...♘e7-d5?.

27 ♖xd7!! ♔xd7 28 ♖b4 ♕xb4

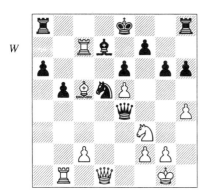

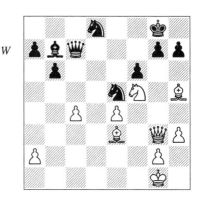

Anand – P. Nikolić
Groningen FIDE KO Wch 1997

Palliser – H. Hunt
British League (4NCL) 1998/9

After 28...♕f5, 29 g4! traps Black's queen.

29 ♗xb4 ♖hc8 30 ♗d6 ♖c4 31 ♘d2 ♖d4 32 c3 ♖d3 33 c4!

Breaking up Black's queenside pawns and getting White's pieces into action against the black king.

33...♖xd2

Or 33...bxc4 34 ♕a4+ ♔d8 35 ♘xc4, when Black is not long for this world.

34 ♕xd2 bxc4 35 ♕xh6

And not before time, Black called it a day.

As the following example shows, one shouldn't think that it is only the super-GMs that have the opportunity to shine. However, the difference is that White didn't play the key move! Black had just played 24...♘e6x♖d8, to which White now replied with the quite reasonable 25 ♗d4 and the game was eventually drawn. At the time my team-mate Jonathan Parker pointed

out the winning move, which Harriet Hunt said after the game she had seen immediately after playing her 24th move. Can you see it?

25 ♗f7+!!

This type of tactic, putting a piece *en prise* on an unoccupied square, can be very difficult to see.

25...♕xf7

After 25...♔xf7?, 26 ♕xg7+ ♔e8 27 ♕xc7 decides the game, while other captures on f7 allow 26 ♕xg7#.

26 ♘h6+ ♔f8 27 ♘xf7

White should go on to win.

One of the things that impresses me about Harriet as a player is her ice-cold approach to the game. Despite having seen 25 ♗f7+ as soon as she had played her mistaken recapture on move 24, she sat at the board for some minutes waiting for her opponent's reply without any signs of a care in the world. Too many players I know would have given the game away either by an audible groan or by their body language. Speelman told me in a similar situation from one of his games he couldn't face staying at the board and had to stay at a distance, nervously awaiting a reply.

This sacrifice on an empty square reminded me of the following game:

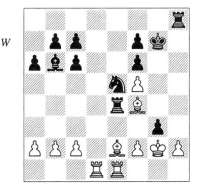

Kasparov – Short
London PCA Wch (17) 1993

Black had just played 23...h4x♘g3. White continued 24 fxg3? allowing 24...♗f2! 25 ♔xf2 ♖xh2+ when Black held an edge although the game was eventually drawn. The difficult thing to see here is that Black sacrifices his bishop on an empty square; the combination 24 hxg3? ♗xf2! 25 ♔xf2 ♖h2+ (reaching the same position) is easier to see. White should instead play 24 ♗xg3, when he holds a small advantage.

A more common version of putting a piece on an unoccupied square would be the following, when the idea is

much more visually obvious and requires little in the way of calculation:

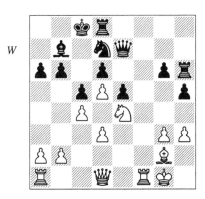

S. Williams – Cherniaev
Hastings Challengers 1998/9

Black has just recaptured a bishop on h6 (17...♖h8x♗h6). White now wrapped things up with **18 ♖f7!**, as Black must lose his queen due to 19 ♘xd6+.

Now and then a game comes along which not only entertains the crowd but makes us stand back in awe. I shall now present two recent examples.

G. Flear – B. Kelly
British League (4NCL) 1998/9

1 d4 d5 2 c4 c6 3 ♘c3 ♘f6 4 e3

This can lead to fairly tame positions. White has now, at least temporarily, locked in his dark-squared bishop, but in the other hand, makes ...dxc4 a less appealing idea for Black since White could recapture without any loss of time.

4...e6 5 ♘f3 ♘bd7 6 ♕c2 ♗d6 7 ♗d2 0-0 8 0-0-0!? *(D)*

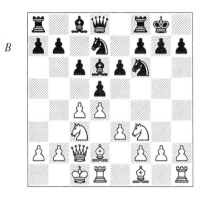

This sharpens things up considerably as with opposite-side castling the game takes a different slant. Glenn obviously wants to play the position *à la* Kasparov, trusting in dynamic play for an advantage and, to be fair, for some time White's pieces seem the more active.

8...a6 9 e4 dxe4 10 ♘xe4 ♘xe4 11 ♕xe4 c5!

A natural attempt to hit back at the centre and try to gain counterchances against White's king by opening up the c-file.

12 ♗c3 ♕e7 13 dxc5?!

Maybe the immediate 13 ♗d3 is better, hoping that Black will choose to exchange on d4 himself, when White can get another piece into the centre with gain of time, i.e. by ♘xd4.

13...♗xc5 14 ♗d3

White's position looks very threatening and his last move forces Black to make a concession on the kingside which leaves him potentially weak,

especially on e6 and the a2-g8 diagonal.

14...f5 15 ♕e2 b5!

Suddenly Black appears to have some play of his own.

16 ♖he1

Of course White has no intention of 'wasting time' by grabbing a pawn on the queenside, as this would just accelerate Black's attacking chances.

16...♘b6 17 g4! *(D)*

That's the side White wants to play on. Both sides have played the position very thematically.

17...bxc4 18 ♗xf5! ♘a4!

The striking thing to me about this game was that each move played appeared to give that player the advantage ... until I saw the opponent's reply! This is typically the type of position I am quite capable of losing from either side!

19 ♗d4!

The combination 19 ♗xh7+? is unsound. After 19...♔xh7 20 ♕e4+ (20 ♕c2+ ♔g8 21 ♕xa4 ♖xf3 leaves Black well on top) 20...♔g8 21 ♕xa8

♘xc3 22 bxc3 ♗b7 23 ♖xe6 ♗xa8 24 ♖xe7 ♗xe7 Black is winning.

19...c3! *(D)*

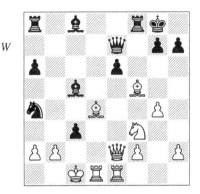

Again the most active and testing move; Black plays for activity with the idea of diverting White's attention from his own attacking possibilities.

20 ♕c4?!

This looks tempting as it hits the knight on a4 and pins Black's e-pawn. However, the tide is turning in Black's favour.

20...♕b7!

Ignoring White's threats by attacking both b2 and f3 simultaneously. For the first time it seems clear that Black is well in control of the situation. 20...♗xd4?! is inferior, because 21 ♖xd4 cxb2+ 22 ♔b1 ♘c5 causes Black's attack to fizzle out.

21 ♗xc3 ♘xc3 22 ♕xc3 exf5!

The attempt to 'win' the exchange by 22...♗b4?! is fraught with danger, e.g. 23 ♗xh7+ ♔h8 (23...♔xh7?! 24 ♕c2+ g6 25 ♘g5+ ♔h8 26 ♖e3 ♕g7 27 ♖h3+ ♔g8 28 ♔b1 and, despite his extra material, it is not clear how

Black should proceed) 24 ♕e5 and if Black is now obliged to take on h7 he is in deep trouble.

23 ♕c4+ ♔h8?!

For the first time Black plays inaccurately. 23...♕f7! 24 ♕xc5 ♗b7 25 ♕a3 ♗xf3 26 ♕xf3 ♕xa2 27 ♕d5+ ♕xd5 28 ♖xd5 fxg4 would have given White a more difficult defensive task.

24 ♕xc5 ♗e6 25 ♕a3!

After 25 ♘d4? ♖ac8 26 ♘xe6 ♖xc5+ 27 ♘xc5 ♕c7 28 ♖d5 fxg4 it's difficult to believe that White has enough resources to hold the position.

25...♗d5

25...♗xa2! leaves White with severe problems.

26 ♘d4 fxg4 27 ♖e7!

Gaining time by putting a rook on the seventh is a prelude to White's 29th move.

27...♕b6 28 ♘c2 ♕c6

28...♖ac8?! intending to meet 29 ♖xd5 by 29...♖xf2 30 ♕c3 ♖xc2+ 31 ♔xc2 (31 ♕xc2?? loses outright to 31...♕g1+) 31...♖xc3+ 32 bxc3 may actually be in White's favour.

29 ♕c3!

Typical of Glenn – in the face of adversity he coolly exchanges into an ending in which Black will find it difficult to generate any real winning chances.

29...♕xc3 30 bxc3 ♖f7

30...♗xa2 seems the last chance for Black to try to claim anything from the position.

31 ♖xf7 ♗xf7 32 ♘e3 ½-½

A fascinating tussle with a result that reflects both players resourceful and enterprising play.

The second was this incredible offering from Kasparov. We join the game after 16...♘d7-b6.

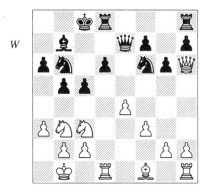

Kasparov – Topalov
Wijk aan Zee 1999

White appears to have a slight edge despite his poorly placed bishop on f1. This is mainly due to Black's king having too much space around it. Having said that, no one could have expected White's violent attack, which drove the enemy king forward into the heart of the white position and finally to its doom.

17 g3

At last allowing his bishop to develop some activity along the h3-c8 diagonal.

17...♔b8 18 ♘a5

Now White's knight goes to a nice outpost on a5 from where it can leer at the black king. Normally I might well have given White's last two moves an '!' but with what is to follow I felt that it might wear out my '!' button!

18...♗a8 19 ♗h3 d5!?

This seems to ask for trouble but may be best. After 19...♖he8 White retains a pleasant edge.

20 ♕f4+ ♔a7 21 ♖he1 d4

This move keeps the position closed and appears solid. However, it allows White to blast the game open in a quite remarkable way.

21...dxe4!? seems to go against the grain, as it opens up the position. However, it isn't obvious to me how White should proceed.

22 ♘d5 ♘bxd5 23 exd5 ♕d6 (D)

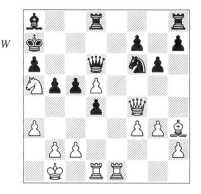

24 ♖xd4!!

The start of some dazzling play.

24...cxd4

24...♔b6! appears to offer White no more than equality after 25 ♘b3 ♗xd5.

25 ♖e7+!

The 'obvious' follow-up.

25...♔b6!

25...♕xe7?? fails to 26 ♕xd4+ ♔b8 27 ♕b6+ ♗b7 (27...♕b7 28 ♘c6#) 28 ♘c6+ ♔a8 29 ♕a7#, while after 25...♔b8 26 ♕xd4 White's attack crashes through, e.g. 26...♘d7 27

♗xd7 ♗xd5 28 ♖xf7!! and Black is completely tied up.

26 ♕xd4+ ♔xa5

Instead 26...♕c5? 27 ♕xf6+ ♔d6 28 ♕xf7 leaves Black with an upward struggle as 28...♔xa5 29 ♖e6! wins the queen, since if it leaves the third rank, 30 b4+ ♔a4 31 ♖xa6# is mate.

27 b4+ ♔a4 28 ♕c3! ♕xd5

28...♗xd5? is met by 29 ♔b2!!, when Black cannot avoid White playing ♕b3+ and after ...♗xb3, cxb3# is mate!

29 ♖a7 ♗b7 30 ♖xb7! ♕c4

Or 30...♖d6 31 ♖b6!! ♖xb6 32 ♔b2, etc.

31 ♕xf6 ♔xa3

31...♖d1+ 32 ♔b2 ♖a8 33 ♕b6 ♕d4+ (after 33...a5, 34 ♗d7! is devastating) 34 ♕xd4 ♖xd4 35 ♖xf7 leaves Black with an uphill struggle.

32 ♕xa6+ ♔xb4 *(D)*

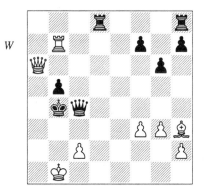

33 c3+!!

Even better than 33 ♗d7, which is also strong. Besides, I expect that by now Kasparov was playing for the crowd.

33...♔xc3 34 ♕a1+ ♔d2

34...♔b4 35 ♕b2+ ♔c5 (35...♕b3? 36 ♖xb5+ wins easily while 35...♔a5 36 ♕a3+ ♕a4 37 ♖a7+ ♔b6 38 ♖xa4 is also straightforward) 36 ♖c7+ ♔d5 37 ♖xc4 bxc4 38 ♕b7+ will decide the issue.

35 ♕b2+ ♔d1 *(D)*

After 35...♔e1 36 ♖e7+ ♔d1 37 ♗f1!! ♖d2 White's simplest course is to transpose to the game by 38 ♖d7.

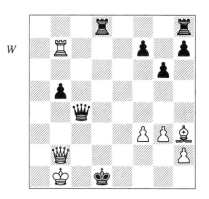

36 ♗f1!! ♖d2

36...♔e1 37 ♗xc4 ♖d1+ 38 ♔a2 ♖a8+ 39 ♔b3 bxc4+ 40 ♔xc4 gets Black nowhere.

37 ♖d7!! ♖xd7 38 ♗xc4 bxc4 39 ♕xh8

White must now just use a modicum of technique.

39...♖d3 40 ♕a8 c3 41 ♕a4+ ♔e1 42 f4 f5 43 ♔c1 ♖d2 44 ♕a7 1-0

Bolts from the Blue – Exercises

The first ten problems are very much White/Black to play and win and are more or less in ascending order of difficulty. The last two require much more calculation and should keep you busy for a while! Solutions on pages 139-41.

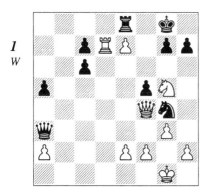

1
W

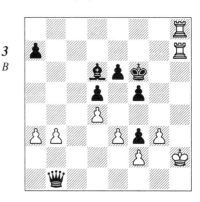

3
B

White to move. A standard mate.

Black to move. White has just coordinated his rooks and seems set to consolidate his position. However, Black now unleashes a bombshell...

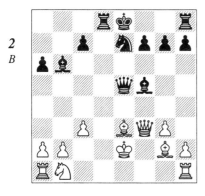

2
B

4
W

Black to move. Find the move that caused White to resign!

In this normal-looking King's Indian position, White came up with a decisive sacrifice; what was it?

5
W

How can White (to play) make use of the h-file to get at the black king?

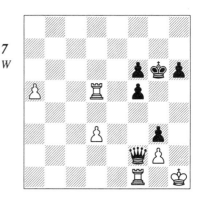

7
W

White to play. The black queen appears immune since the f-pawn looks unstoppable if White captures on f2. However, appearances can be deceptive!

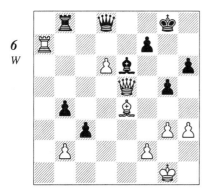

6
W

How should White (to play) exploit the draughty-looking situation of the black king?

8
W

White to move. The first move may be relatively obvious, but can you see the conclusion before playing it on the board? Don't be afraid to invest material in a good cause!

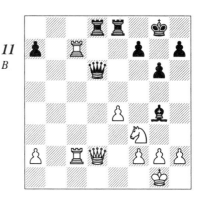

White to move. The first move is fairly natural but the follow-up is unusual to say the least!

How can Black (to play) exploit the potential weakness of White's back rank?

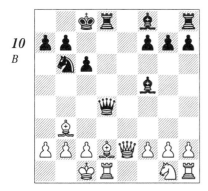

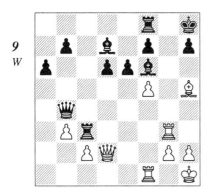

Black to move. Again the initial move is a fairly standard idea against a king which has castled queenside but the follow-up is a real stunner!

Black to play. Despite his extra two pawns, the win is by no means trivial due to the bishops of opposite colour. How did Black convert his advantage into a win? The key move is possibly the last move you would consider!

17 Chess and Computers

Twenty-five years ago chess computers were in their infancy and even the most enlightened found it hard to believe that a computer would be able to beat an accomplished player within their lifetime. In fact, until relatively recently, the Scottish international master David Levy had a standing bet that he would play any computer in a match for £10,000. However, he eventually had to give way to the inevitable (but at least by that time inflation had caught up with the size of the bet involved!).

During the 1990s, the best computers have become challenging opponents even for strong grandmasters, with even the great Kasparov losing a match, albeit under somewhat odd circumstances, to Deep Blue in 1997.

Now, even modestly priced systems can hold their own, especially at blitz, with the most able players. Moreover, computers have had an even more profound impact on chess as assistants to human players. Sophisticated database management systems have been developed to handle vast quantities of games, providing players with a wealth of information at their fingertips. How to get the most out of these database programs shall be my main topic in this chapter. After all, it is no use having a 'nice car' if you don't know how to drive!

Chess-Playing Computers

Firstly, though, I would like to make a few points about computers as players. The first decision to be made is whether to buy a dedicated chess-playing computer, or a playing program for use on a PC. A few issues to consider are:

1) A PC can be used for other purposes (games such as Doom and FIFA '98, or serious items such as word-processing, accounting, etc.).

2) If you already have a PC you can cut down on cost or get more for your money by getting a chess-playing program for it.

3) A chess-playing computer is generally more portable (unless you have a small laptop PC).

4) A PC program tends to have a better display in terms of the information it provides. For instance, the more advanced programs tend to have coaching facilities, provide running assessments of lines they are analysing, a display of their 'opening book', etc., and thus are more user-friendly.

5) The playing strength of programs that run on a PC will depend on the speed of your processor and the RAM that is available; when you upgrade your hardware, you are in effect

also upgrading your chess-playing program. A reasonable Pentium system with 32MB of RAM should provide a very tough opponent for anyone.

I must confess that I have little knowledge of what is available in terms of dedicated chess-playing computers, as I have little interest in them myself. Looking in a recent catalogue, though, they appear to range from £90 (c. $150) for a simple handheld machine to £450 (c. $720) for a table-top machine with a high-quality sensory board (I am assuming that you want a machine that plays very good chess; there are cheaper computers that are suitable for novices). These will no doubt offer an excellent game to 90% of club players.

However, it must be said that the display on a VDU combined with the excellent 'coach' display on, for example, Fritz (a leading PC program) is invaluable. With a chess-playing program, you will normally get extra options. For example, you can alter the design/size of the board, flip position (so that you can always view the position from your perspective) and get a clear visual display of the analysis of the position if you want it. If you decide to opt for a chess-playing program, then one option is to go for the latest version of Fritz (at the time of writing, this is Fritz 5.32, the 32-bit version of the popular Fritz 5 program), as this will give you both a 'playing partner' and a reasonably powerful database management system. Moreover, Fritz is designed to link in to ChessBase...

Database Management Systems

Before going into the types/usage, something should be said in regard to your computer itself. As with chess playing programs, the processor speed and the RAM available will affect the efficiency and speed of what you are doing. For normal work with a chess database program, any decent Pentium will do the job nicely, though if you want to work with very large databases or use the more advanced functions, the more powerful your machine, and the larger your hard disk, the better.

If you have an Apple Macintosh, I am afraid the bad news is that there isn't very much chess software available. You will be able to find some chess-playing programs, and some relatively rudimentary database tools, but the major programs are currently PC only.

There are a number of systems available but for practical purposes I shall spend time showing you some of the things that ChessBase can do, as this is the most sophisticated program, and the one I use myself. ChessBase starts at less than £200 for the basic package. Once you have the program, future upgrades to the latest version are much more modestly priced, e.g. from ChessBase 6.0 to version 7.0 costs about £90 (c. $145).

One of the most useful things about modern database programs is that you can call up an analysis engine, such as Fritz or Junior, to analyse in the background, constantly displaying its analysis and assessment of the position you are looking at. However, when you buy a database program you don't necessarily get an analysis engine as part of the basic package, so check whether you need to pay extra for one. (In case you are getting confused by the references to 'Fritz', I should explain that this is the name used not only for the engine that analyses and assesses positions, but also for the program that, amongst other things, enables you to play against this engine. Both ChessBase and the Fritz program can also use alternative engines.) To buy the Fritz program will cost about £90 (c. $145), but you will get several engines for this price, and upgrades to future versions, as for ChessBase, will cost substantially less.

The other main issue pricewise is that the that basic packages will come with only a small database of games. The important thing with game databases is to get quality rather than just quantity and from this viewpoint the Mega Database (compiled by Chess-Base) can come highly recommended, but it is expensive. I use this together with TWIC (The Week In Chess, edited by Mark Crowther) more than anything else. TWIC can be downloaded from the Internet on a weekly basis, and is free. Normally, data that is freely available on the Internet should be viewed with suspicion (download it by all means, but keep it completely separate from your high-quality data), but TWIC data is on the whole very reliable.

Now we come to the 'nitty-gritty': once you have a computer, a database management system, some game databases and an analysis engine (or two!), what can you do with it?

There are of course numerous functions but I will try to cover what I consider to be generally the most useful. For this purpose I will use ChessBase 7 as the example.

Getting the most out of your database

Form a database of your own games to store them for reference and to play through them, with the analysis engine running. From this you can try to find out exactly where things went wrong; often you may have considered your position to be tenable far longer than it actually was and only noticed the 'symptoms' of the previous error rather than the error itself. Then cross-reference your game from the last point you know was theory against your big databases to see what has been played (preferably by well-known, strong players), the results they got in this line and the ideas they played. This enables you to repair the damage done, ready for the next time you play the line.

It can be useful to form smaller databases of games specifically in the opening variations you play, as this reduces the time needed to search for games and positions. However, this is only useful if you keep these databases up to date (which requires some dedication), and are sure that the openings key you are using to select the games is sufficiently detailed for the purpose.

There are two straightforward ways of **searching for game by a particular player**. Firstly from the database window, you can press the button with the player's face on it (is this Kasparov?) and select the name from the letters offered. The one thing to be careful about here is that players may have entries of their games under several different spellings, e.g. C.Baker, C.W.Baker, Chris Baker or Chris W. Baker, while looking up Korchnoi (the standard English-language transliteration of his name; there are a couple of dozen other versions in wide use though) can prove a nightmare. In a high-quality database, the spellings of names should have been standardized, so this method gives more satisfactory results.

The second method is to go into the database itself and use the search mask facility. The main advantage of this is that you can narrow down the search if you are looking for something more specific, i.e. his games in a certain year, as White or Black, playing against opponents of a certain minimum rating, in specific openings, etc. Searching for a player's games is of course invaluable in opening preparation prior to the game itself, and ChessBase 7.0 has a very useful Player Profile function that will provide all the information you should need, i.e. ratings over recent years, openings played by code, performance within these variations and of course his games.

You can **search for a position** by entering the preceding moves if it is for an opening position or by setting up the position from scratch if it is from a middlegame/endgame position.

The **opening keys** are very useful for getting an overview of an opening or for finding games in particular variations. You can also modify the keys yourself, for instance to add further detail in lines you play. It is also possible to create your own opening keys from scratch.

You can search for a position not only in the database you are currently working but also across as many other databases as you choose.

A very powerful feature is the facility to **merge** games together. Chess-Base will compare the games being merged, and find the latest moments at which they had the same position, and merge them together so that one game is the main game and the other(s) are inserted as variations in the notes to that game.

A game with notes (such as those produced when merging games) can be converted to a table format, which can be printed out if you wish.

In ChessBase 7.0 you can get a 'tree' of moves played in a position showing the moves played, the Elo performance produced by each move and the number of times each move has been tried. In this way you can identify the most important lines.

You can print out games, diagrams and analysis for your own use or training/writing purposes, or 'cut and paste' them into a word processing program.

I find one little 'extra' on Chess-Base 7.0 particularly nice in that it displays clearly in one box any material imbalance in the position you are looking at – this can help reorientate you in a position where there have been several sacrifices.

This is a summary of what I find most useful myself although there are numerous other functions, some of which you may find of great benefit.

I would like to move on now to some practical examples of how a computer can be used to work on a game but also to show some of the things that you must be careful about. For these examples I have used ChessBase 7.0 with a Fritz 5 engine on a laptop PC with 64 MB of RAM and a 300 MHz '3D Now!' processor, generally giving the machine a few minutes in critical positions.

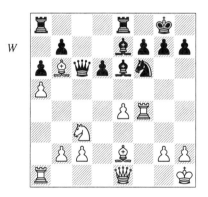

Plaskett – Mordue
Clevedon 1998

18 ♗d4

Here previously only 18 ♕g3 had been played – Fritz assessed this as ± 0.44. This means Fritz believes that White is 0.44 'pawns' ahead, which would seem reasonable and quite normal for a standard opening position. I would like to add a note of caution here in that I wouldn't worry about a few hundredths of a pawn; it takes more than that to win a game!

18...♘d7 19 ♘d5!?

Fritz is quite rightly unsure about this move. Another thing that is typical of computers is that they like material. The fact that Fritz thinks the position is 'about equal' despite Black being a pawn ahead means that it thinks White has about a 'pawn's worth' of compensation.

19...♗xd5 20 exd5 ♕xc2

This is almost certainly safer than 20...♕xd5. It would be risky for Black to open up the a2-g8 diagonal when he is missing his light-squared bishop.

21 ♕g3

21 ♖c1!? seems natural but then Black has 21...♗h4!, which was the move Mordue intended, and considered strong. However, Fritz came up with the amazing 22 ♖xf7!?, but after the calm 22...♕g6! 23 ♖xg7+ ♕xg7 24 ♕xh4 the position remains unclear. This is the kind of position where Fritz excels – 22 ♖xf7!? is not the kind of move that instantly springs to mind!

21...♘e5 22 ♗h5 ♖f8

Fritz suggested 22...g6 here, but I find that a little too weakening for my taste.

23 ♖af1 f5!?

Found instantly as best by Fritz but Mordue said that he had to invest some time before judging this as the correct way to continue.

24 ♗d1 ♛c7

Fritz suggests 24...♛d2 as best but I think the text-move is a sensible retreat.

25 ♖xf5

Fritz for once preferred not winning the pawn back, but instead playing 25 ♗c3, maintaining the pressure.

25...♖xf5

Black chooses to release some of the tension by exchanging rooks. Fritz offered 25...♛c4 threatening ...♛xf1+.

26 ♖xf5 ♖f8 27 ♖xf8+

27 ♛c3! straight away may be slightly more accurate, as Fritz points out, as f7 would no longer be available to the black queen.

27...♗xf8 28 ♛c3 ♛f7

It is necessary for Black to keep the queens on, since the ending would be very unpleasant for Black in practice. Fritz, however, considers the queen exchange 'academically best'. This may be true but things such as time-control and practical play, further inaccuracies, etc., are not a consideration for Fritz.

29 ♔g1 ♛f4 30 ♛e3?! ♛f5?!

Here Fritz quickly points out that the time may have been right to exchange, as after 30...♛xe3+ 31 ♗xe3 ♘c4 Black wins a pawn although I'm sure White has enough resources to hold the balance.

31 ♗e2

31 b3! may be more solid.

31...♛b1+ 32 ♗f1 ♗e7

After 32...♛a2!? 33 ♗xe5 dxe5 34 ♛xe5 ♛xa5 Black's position may well be defensible, although I would still prefer to be White.

33 ♛h3! ♛c1 34 ♛e6+ ♔f8 35 ♛f5+

After 35 ♗xe5 dxe5, 36 ♛xe5?? ♗c5+ would have been sad.

35...♗f6 36 ♗c3 ♛e3+ 37 ♔h1 ♛c5

The position is now unclear, but it is White who has the chances.

38 h3 h6 39 ♗e2!? ♛xd5 40 ♗f3 ♛c4 41 ♗xb7 ♔e7 42 ♛c8?!

Giving up any intentions of playing for the win.

42...♛f1+ 43 ♔h2 ♛f4+ 44 ♔h1

Fritz was quick to point out that if White tries to avoid the perpetual with 44 ♔g1? he will soon get into trouble after 44...♗h4!, viz. 45 ♛c7+ ♘d7 46 ♛c6 ♛f2+ 47 ♔h1 ♛f1+ 48 ♔h2 ♗f2 and White will have to play 49 h4 and keep his fingers crossed.

44...♛f1+ 45 ♔h2 ♛f4+ 46 ♔h1
½-½

Fritz still hasn't learnt to take into consideration things like the fact that Jim was half a point ahead going into this final round or his desire to score 100% for the Grand Prix points with only a month to go, but then they're the kind of things that separate us from machines!

What did impress me was that nearly every move played, apart from the inaccuracies, were considered by Fritz, and that Fritz found some of the 'difficult' moves almost instantly.

The next example though, which comes from one of Tyson Mordue's postal games, shows how you need to be careful in taking what Fritz says as 'gospel'.

1 e4 ♘f6 2 e5 ♘d5 3 d4 d6 4 ♘f3 g6 5 ♗c4 ♘b6 6 ♗b3 ♗g7 7 ♘g5 e6 8 ♕f3 0-0

This obvious and natural move is not so common in this position; 8...♕e7 is more usual.

9 ♕h3 h6 10 ♘f3

White has done better with 10 ♘e4, and this is the main reason for Black avoiding 8...0-0.

10...dxe5 11 dxe5

After 11 ♗xh6?! exd4 12 ♗xg7 (12 ♗g5 e5! is fine for Black) 12...♔xg7 Black is doing nicely.

11...c5! *(D)*

Previously, 11...♘c6 had almost invariably been played, but the text-move seems like a very sensible alternative.

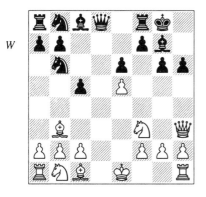

12 ♗xh6

12 c3 was actually played in the game, and rated as ± 0.56 by Fritz. However, the text-move, 12 ♗xh6, was given as ± 0.59 after an initially

high +− evaluation. From now on I will give Fritz's analysis as to the best moves for each side, together with its evaluations.

12...c4

= 0.00!

13 ♗e3

∓ −0.34! Originally Fritz had intended 13 ♘g5 but now had gone off the idea.

13...f6

∓ −0.25.

14 ♗xb6

∓ −0.22.

14...♕xb6

−+ −1.25. Although still highly complex, further analysis seems only to reinforce the view that Black now stands better.

So where did White go wrong after 12 ♗xh6? The answer is probably that he didn't, but that the initial ± 0.59 was incorrect. As stated in the note to 13 ♗e3, Fritz had originally intended 13 ♘g5 but had seen a flaw at that point, and so had to change direction. This leads to an interesting question – do computers follow a plan through to its logical conclusion? The answer, of course, is that they do not, but will simply play what they consider to be the best move as they see that further half-move ahead after each move is actually played. If this is the case, how useful are computers for developing a player's strategic planning? The important lesson is that one mustn't place blind faith in a computer's assessment, but to make sure that it has enough time in critical positions, and to verify its recommendations by giving the computer time to look at critical positions that arise at a later point in the lines it is advocating.

Finally though, to balance the books, I will give an example from one of my half-hour rapid-play games I recently played as Black.

1 e4 e5 2 d4 exd4 3 ♕xd4 ♘c6 4 ♕e3 ♗b4+

To be honest I made this up over the board to avoid too much opening preparation, although Mark Hebden told me afterwards it was a good alternative to the main line. The idea is to meet 5 c3 with 5...♗e7, when, although Black has lost a tempo, he has taken away the natural developing square, c3, from White's knight.

5 ♘c3 ♘f6

Unbeknown to me (ignorance is bliss) I had transposed back to the main line of this somewhat obscure opening. 5...♘ge7 is a way to avoid this.

6 ♗d2 0-0 7 0-0-0 ♖e8 8 ♕g3 ♖xe4

I thought White had missed this and that I already had a good position. Fritz thought Black was already a little better and considered 9 ♗g5 and 9 h3 as White's best options, although these seem to offer White very little in compensation. 9 a3! is actually considered to be the most dangerous.

9 ♗d3?! ♖g4 10 ♕h3 d5 11 f3 ♖d4 12 ♕g3

12 g4 ♘e5 is strong for Black.

12...♗d6 13 ♕f2 *(D)*

Here, after initially considering the solid but rather uninspiring 13...♗e6 to be best, much to my surprise Fritz came up with the move I chose.

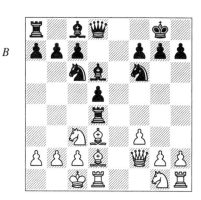

B

13...♖xd3!

I was very pleased with this move. I considered that a pawn, the bishop-pair, White's obvious weakness on d3 and around his king in general, coupled with the fact that White's attacking chances have virtually vanished more than adequately compensated for the minimal material invested. What surprises me though is that after long thought Fritz decided that 13...♖xd3 was best (perhaps for different reasons!). However, it is impressive if Fritz now has some way of 'judging' compensation!

14 cxd3 ♗f5 15 ♗g5 ♘b4 16 ♕e2 h6 17 ♗h4 ♗f4+

Fritz preferred to play the immediate 17...d4.

18 ♔b1 ♕d6 19 ♗xf6

Necessary, because 19...♖e8 would otherwise be an unpleasant move to meet.

19...♕xf6 20 ♔a1?! ♕a6!

The pressure on d3 is beginning to tell and ideas of ...d4, exposing the weakness on a2, are also not to be underestimated.

21 ♘h3! ♗d6 22 d4??

The sort of move that half-hour chess is all about!

22...♘c2+ 23 ♔b1 ♘xd4+ 0-1

In summary, I think programs like ChessBase are invaluable to both preparation and personal development. Maybe I'm biased but in the 11 months since I got my first system on a 486, I managed at last to achieve my International Master title at the tender age of 40! The one thing to take into consideration, though, is that the computer should be used to reinforce your ideas and preparation – it is not a substitute for your hard work, thinking and judgement.

Solutions to Exercises

Middlegame Exercises

The notes to these positions are based on those by Alexander Baburin.

1) Krasenkow – Van der Sterren
Groningen FIDE KO Wch 1997

(Black has just played 15...♕d8-e7?. Instead, 15...g6 would have been better.)

16 e4!

Of course Black doesn't want to take the pawn due to 17 ♗d6, but it is still an interesting concept for White to exchange e- for d-pawn. Normally one would expect White to blockade in order to make use of the 'weak' square on d4 followed by long-term piece play against the d5-pawn.

16...♕d8

16...♕d7 is a logical alternative, while 16...♖fd8?! 17 e5 ♕c7! 18 exf6 ♕xf4 19 fxg7 leaves Black's position inferior due to his bad pawn structure and the weakened position of his king.

17 ♕d3!

After 17 e5 ♗e7 18 ♘d4 (not 18 ♕d3 g6 19 ♗h6 ♖e8 20 ♘d4? ♘xe5, when White has insufficient play for the pawn) 18...♘xd4 19 ♕xd4 ♕d7 20 ♕d3 g6 21 ♗h6 ♖fc8 Black has equalized as White has no knight to occupy the blockading square d4 and the plan of f4-f5 is too slow.

17...dxe4 18 ♕xe4 g6 19 ♖fd1

In an open position of this type, White's piece activity guarantees him the advantage; in particular, compare the relative position of both sides' rooks.

19...♕b6 20 ♗e3 ♕c7?!

This is too passive. The critical line is 20...♕b5 21 ♕f4!, when White has attacking chances but there is still a lot of work to be done.

21 ♘g5! ♖fe8

21...♗f5? allows 22 ♕h4 ♗xg5 23 ♗xg5 ♗xb1 24 ♗f6, when Black has problems stopping the invasion of the white queen on the dark squares around his king.

22 ♕h4 h5 23 ♘xe6! ♖xe6 24 ♕c4

The bishop-pair gives White the initiative in this type of position.

24...♕e7 25 ♗a2 ♗g5 26 ♗xg5?!

White could retain the bishops and get an even better position than in the game with 26 ♗c5! ♕f6 27 ♖b1 ♖ae8 28 ♕f1.

26...♕xg5 27 f4 ♕f6?

A tactical mistake. 27...♕e7 is necessary.

28 ♕c5! ♖e7?

28...♖e2 is better.

29 ♖d6 ♕xf4 30 ♖f1 ♕e4 31 ♗d5 ♕d4+ 32 ♕xd4 ♘xd4 33 ♖xg6+ ♔h7 34 ♖b6

Now White has a distinct advantage owing to his well-placed rooks, better minor piece and superior pawn-structure.

2) J. Polgar – Anand
Wijk aan Zee 1998

14 ♗g5!

The main idea behind this move is simple: eliminate Black's knights and gain control of the d5-square.

14...♖fc8 15 ♘e1

The strength of this move is that it reduces the chances of Black gaining counterplay down the c-file against c2. This is often a compensating factor for the potential weaknesses caused when playing the earlier ...e5.

15...♕b7 16 ♗xf6 ♘xf6 17 ♘d5 ♘xd5 18 ♖xd5 ♖c5 19 ♖ad1 ♖xd5 20 ♖xd5 ♖c8

20...b4 must have come into consideration as it makes it very difficult for White to advance her c-pawn. However, it does concede control of more light squares. For instance, the new 'outpost' on c4 would be a very tempting square for the white knight.

21 c3 b4 22 c4 g6 23 g3 ♖c5 24 ♖d1!

Further exchanges could well reduce White's advantage. Moreover, White wants to occupy the d5-square with a piece, rather than a pawn.

24...a5 25 ♘c2 ♔g7 26 ♕d3 ♖c6 27 ♘e3 ♕c8 28 ♔g2 ♕e6 29 ♕e2 ♗d8 30 ♘d5

The knight is a monster with tentacles spreading over all parts of the board, and unfortunately for Black the cost of removing it would be far too high. However, this piece in itself will

not win the game, so White needs to force more weaknesses or conduct an attack. She is helped in this aim by the fact that Black is not well situated to create active counterplay.

30...♖c5 31 ♕e3 ♗e7 32 ♖d3 ♗d8 33 ♕d2 ♖c6 34 ♕d1 ♔g8 35 h4 ♔g7?

Totally passive defence is in this case virtually a sign of capitulation. 35...h5 is necessary.

36 h5!

This probing move adds to the pressure on Black's kingside.

36...♗g5 37 ♕f3 ♖c8 38 ♖d1 ♖c6 39 ♕e2 ♖c8 40 ♖h1 ♔g8 41 f3!

Not only supporting e4 but more importantly freeing the f2-square for the white queen, from where it can infiltrate along the g1-a7 diagonal or conveniently switch to the kingside. There is little chance of Black being able to exploit the slight weakening of White's king.

41...♖b8 42 ♕f2 ♖b7 43 hxg6 fxg6

43...hxg6? allows 44 ♕g1! f5 (or 44...♗f6 45 ♕h2 ♗g7 46 ♕h4 and Black's position is on the verge of collapse) 45 ♕h2 ♗f6 46 ♕h6 and now White will infiltrate, e.g. 46...♗g7 47 ♕g5 ♖d7 48 ♖a1 and Black cannot cope with White's domination on both the a- and h-files.

44 c5!

Finally White breaks through, having pushed Black's pieces onto sensible-looking but inactive squares.

44...dxc5 45 ♕xc5 ♗d8 46 ♖c1 ♔f7 47 ♕e3 ♔g7 48 ♖c4 ♖d7 49 ♕c1 h5 50 ♖c6 ♖d6 51 ♖c8 ♕d7 52 ♕c5 ♔h6 53 ♖b8 ♗f6 54 ♕e3+ ♗g5 55 f4 exf4 56 ♖h8+ 1-0

Black resigned due to the variation 56...♔g7 57 ♕d4+ ♗f6 58 ♕xf6+! ♖xf6 59 ♖h7+ ♔xh7 60 ♘xf6+ and 61 ♘xd7.

3) Kuijf – Shaked
Wijk aan Zee 1998

16 ♘fxe6!!

Blowing apart Black's plan of regrouping his minor pieces prior to completing his development and moving his king to safety.

16...fxe6 17 ♕h5+ g6

Black would like to untangle his pieces and complete his development, but 17...♘g6? meets with a sticky end after 18 ♘xe6 ♕d7 19 ♗xd5 ♗xd5 20 ♕xd5 because of the fork on c7.

18 ♕e5 ♖g8 19 ♗g5!

This natural developing move piles on the pressure to the point where Black's position disintegrates. However, 19 ♘xe6 ♕d7 20 axb4 is also strong.

19...h6

After 19...♗g7 20 ♕xe6 Black is unable to put up any real resistance.

20 ♗xe7 ♘xe7

After 20...♗xe7, 21 ♕xe6 exploits the loose black pieces on c6 and g8.

21 ♗xc6+ ♘xc6 22 ♕xe6+ ♘e7 23 ♘e4 1-0

Very dynamic play by White.

4) Sakaev – Rustemov
Moscow 1998

30 ♗xg6!

30 ♘xg6!, based on the same theme, is also very strong, e.g. 30...hxg6 31

♗xg6 ♕xg3+ 32 ♔xg3 ♘xg6 33 ♕c3, when White ought to be winning easily although the material imbalance makes it a little harder than in the game.

30...hxg6 31 ♘xg6 ♗e6?!

A better try is 31...♕xg3+ 32 ♔xg3 ♘xg6 33 ♕c3, leading to the position in the previous note.

32 ♘h5+ ♔f7 33 ♘hf4!?

Clinically building up the pressure. 33 ♘h8+ ♔g8 34 ♘xf6+ ♔g7 35 ♘xe8+ ♖xe8 is less clear.

33...♖d7 34 ♖h6 ♕c7 35 ♖eh1

White seizes the opportunity to use the h-file to good effect.

35...♕a5 36 ♘xf8 ♖xf8 37 ♖xf6+! ♔e7

After 37...♔xf6 38 ♕g6+ ♔e7 39 ♕xg5+ ♔f7 (39...♔e8 40 ♘xe6 ♕xa2+ 41 ♔g3 and Black is busted) 40 ♘xe6 White will win back at least the exchange, leaving him in a commanding position.

38 ♖xf8 ♔xf8 39 ♖h5 ♘e4+ 40 fxe4 ♗xg4 41 ♖g5 1-0

Black has nothing left to fight for.

5) Vaïsser – Comas Fabrego
New York 1998

(White has just played 23 d5-d6?.)

23...♗xd6 24 ♖d1 ♗xb5 25 ♗xb5

It is not so much Black's extra pawn that matters, but rather control of the light squares.

25...c4!

This move activates Black's bishop and fights for the light squares.

26 ♔h1 ♕e7 27 ♕d2 c3!? 28 bxc3

After 28 ♕xd6 ♕xd6 29 ♖xd6 cxb2 30 ♖g1 ♖c1 31 ♗d3 ♖ac8 32

♖b6 ♖8c3 33 ♖xb7 f6 34 ♖xb2 ♖xg1+ 35 ♔xg1 ♖xd3 36 ♖a2 ♔f7 Black has a very good ending.

28...♗xa3 29 ♕c2 ♗b4 30 ♖xa4 ♖xa4 31 ♕xa4 ♗xc3 32 ♗c4 ♗d4 33 ♕b3 g6

Black keeps an extra pawn in a position where he also has the more active bishop.

34 g3 ♖c5 35 ♔g2 ♕c7 36 ♗d3 ♖c3 37 ♕b5 ♔g7 38 h4 h5 39 ♖b1 b6 40 ♖d1?! ♖c2+! 41 ♔h3 ♕c8+ 42 g4 ♖f2 43 ♗e2 hxg4+ 44 fxg4 ♕c3+ 45 ♗d3 ♗c5 0-1

6) Baburin – Ippolito
Bermuda 1998

(Black has just played 20...♖a8-b8. After the interesting 20...c5!?, White can keep an edge by 21 ♗e4 ♖b8 22 ♕a5!?.)

21 ♘e5!

Not 21 ♘d2? c5! 22 d5 ♕xc3 23 bxc3.

21...♗d6 22 ♗c4 ♗e6 23 ♖xe6! fxe6 24 ♘d7 ♕e7

24...♕f4 25 d5+! e5 26 ♘xb8 ♗xb8 27 dxc6 bxc6 gives White an advantage due to his safer king and fewer weaknesses.

25 d5+ e5

25...♔g8 can be met by 26 dxe6 ♖d8 27 g3!?, with winning chances for White.

26 ♘xb8 ♗xb8 27 dxc6 bxc6

White's structural superiority gives him an excellent game.

28 g3!?

A good practical move, given that Black was in time-trouble: White just improves his position, not rushing into any forcing play just yet.

28...♗c7 29 ♗a2 c5 30 ♕b3 ♕f8 31 ♕e6 ♗b8 32 ♕d7+ ♔h8 33 ♗b1 ♕d6 34 ♕e8+ ♔g7 35 ♗e4?

Instead of this hasty move, White could win by 35 ♗xg6! ♕xg6 (alternatively, 35...♕f8 36 ♕e6 ♕f6 37 ♕d7+! wins) 36 ♕xb8 ♕b1+ 37 ♔g2 ♕e4+ 38 ♔f1 ♕d3+ 39 ♔e1 ♕e4+ 40 ♔d2 ♕d4+ 41 ♔c1.

35...h5 36 h4 ♗c7 37 ♕a8 ♗b6 38 ♗d5 ♕f8 39 ♕b7+ ♔h6 40 ♗c4 ♕f6 41 b3 ♕f8 42 ♔g2 ♕f6 43 a4

With some ideas of playing a5.

43...♕f8 44 ♕d5 ♕f6 45 ♕d7 ♕f8 46 ♕d2+ ♔g7 47 ♕d5 ♕f6 48 ♕d7+ ♔h6 49 ♗g8! ♕h8 50 ♗d5! ♕f6 51 ♗e4 c4 52 ♕d2+ ♔g7 53 bxc4 ♗d4 54 ♕c2 ♕b6?! 55 c5! ♗xc5 56 ♗xg6 ♗xf2?

After 56...♕xg6 57 ♕xc5 ♕e4+ 58 ♔h2 ♕xa4 59 ♕xe5+ ♔g8 60 ♕g5+ ♔f8 61 ♕xh5 a5 White should win, but it is more complex.

57 ♗xh5 ♗d4 58 ♗f3 ♕d6 59 ♗e4 ♗b6 60 ♕d3 ♗d4 61 ♕e2 ♕d7 62 ♕a6 ♕f7 63 ♕b7 ♕xb7 64 ♗xb7 a5 65 ♗e4 ♗c3 66 g4 ♗e1 67 ♔h3 ♗f2 68 g5 ♗e3 69 ♔g4 ♗f4 70 h5 ♗e3 71 h6+ ♔f7 72 g6+ 1-0

Endgame Exercises

Notes to endings 4-7 are based on those by Hans-Joachim Hecht.

1) Baker – Lilley
Hanham 1997

32 ♖f6! g5 33 ♖f5 g4 34 ♖g5 g3

34...♖b4 35 ♔f2 and ♔g3 picks up the g-pawn.

35 ♖xg3 ♖xg3 36 hxg3

The ending king and two doubled pawns vs king is always won in this type of situation as you can 'lose' a move with the second pawn if necessary to gain (or regain) the opposition.

36...♔f7 37 ♔f2 ♔g6 38 ♔f3 ♔f5 39 g4+ ♔g5 40 ♔g3 ♔g6 41 ♔f4 ♔f6 42 g5+ ♔g6 43 ♔g4 ♔g7 44 ♔f5 ♔f7 45 g6+ ♔g8 46 ♔f6 ♔f8 47 g7+ ♔g8 48 g3 1-0

2) C. Morris – Baker
Cardiff 1998

38...♖a2! 39 h4

39 h3 leads to a similar conclusion.

39...♖a3 40 ♖g5 h6! 41 ♖g4?

The situation was hopeless anyway as without ♖g4 the g-pawn would have fallen.

41...♖a4+ 0-1

3) Baker – Conquest
British League (4NCL) 1997/8

33 ♘e4! ♗xf3

After 33...♗c7 34 ♖e3 White is just a sound pawn ahead.

34 ♘xd6 ♗xd5 35 ♘xe8 ♗xc4 36 a3 bxa3 37 bxa3

A draw was soon agreed.

4) Smagin – Ilinčić
Belgrade-Moscow, Belgrade 1998

39...♖xe3+!

The simplest, and most fool-proof way to win is to simplify into a king

and pawn ending. Black could undoubtedly win the rook vs knight ending by a plan such as ...♖b1, ...♔d2-e1 and ...♖b2, but that allows more scope for something to go wrong.

40 fxe3 e5 41 h4 h5 42 g4 e4+ 0-1

5) And. Rodriguez – Zarnicki
Villa Gisell 1998

(White has just played 53 ♔e3-d4. If instead 53 ♔f4, Black could reach a winning pawn ending by 53...♖f6 54 ♔e5 ♖xf5+ 55 ♔xf5 ♔h4 56 ♔f6 {or 56 ♔e5 ♔xh3 57 ♔d5 h5 58 ♔c5 h4 59 ♔xb5 ♔g3 60 ♔a6 h3 61 b5 h2 62 b6 h1♕ with a won queen vs pawn ending} 56...♔xh3 57 ♔g5 ♔g3 and Black wins.)

53...♖c6 54 ♘e3 ♔h4 55 ♔d5 ♖c8 56 ♘f5+ ♔xh3 57 ♘d6 ♖d8!

Thus Black forces the same liquidation to a king and pawn ending as described above.

58 ♔c6 ♖xd6+ 59 ♔xd6 ♔g4 60 ♔c6 h5 61 ♔xb5 h4 62 ♔a6 h3 63 b5 h2 64 b6 h1♕ 0-1

6) Schmaltz – Onishchuk
New York 1998

60...a5+!

Black 'changes' his advantage by liquidating to a king and pawn ending which is won due to his outside passed pawn.

61 ♘xa5 ♗xc5+ 62 ♔xc5

Otherwise Black wins with his two connected passed pawns.

62...b6+ 63 ♔b4 bxa5+ 64 ♔xa5 ♔d6 65 ♔b6 ♔e5 66 ♔xc6 ♔f4 0-1

Black wins after 67 ♔d5 ♔xf3 68 ♔e6 ♔xe4 69 ♔xf6 ♔f4.

7) **Ivanchuk – Kramnik**
Linares 1998

51...c4!! 52 bxc4 ♖d2+ Black picks
After 52 ♗xc4 ♖d2+ Black picks up the c- and a-pawns.

52...♖b8 53 c5 ♖b2 54 c6 ♔e7 55 ♘xg6+ ♔d6 56 ♘e5 ♖xa2 57 ♘c4+ ♔c7

57...♔xc6 is also sufficient.

58 ♔g3

58 ♗xf5?? loses to 58...♖xc2+!.

58...♖a1

Not 58...♖xc2? 59 ♘xa3 ♖c3? 60 ♘b5+.

59 ♘xa3 ♖xa3 60 ♔h4 ♔xc6 61 ♔g5 ♖a5 62 ♗xf5 ♔d6 63 ♔g4 ♔e7 64 ♗d3 ♖c5 65 ♔f3 ♔d6 66 ♔e4 ♖h5 67 c4 ♖h4 68 ♔f5 ♔c5 69 ♔e5 ♖h3 70 ♔e4 ♖h4 71 ♗e2 ♖h2 72 ♔f3 ♔d4 73 ♗f1 ♖h1 74 ♔f2 ♖h8 ½-½

8) **Runau – Meštrović**
Hastings 1971/2

1 ♔g4 ♔e6

Now 2 ♔xh4? ♔f5 3 ♔g3 is only a draw after 3...g5 4 fxg5 ♔xg5.

2 ♔h3! 1-0

After 2...♔f5 3 ♔xh4 it is Black's king which must retreat, allowing 4 ♔g5 and an easy win.

Knowing the Rules

1) Think to yourself 'nice try' and point out that he has already moved his king (twice!), and, more importantly, insist, in some ways, that he moves his king.

2) Stop the clock and call in the controller. I would expect the controller to warn your opponent about not changing the pawn for the appropriate piece, award you extra time on your clock for the disturbance of your concentration and insist, seeing as the piece wasn't placed on the board correctly, that it must be assumed to be promoted to a queen.

3) You can accept the draw if you wish (!) or, as Black's claim was improperly executed (you must write down the move and claim the draw without actually playing it on the board), play either **6 ♔g1** or **6 ♔g2** (either would be for only the second time) intending to meet **6...♕g4+** with **7 ♗g3+** and the expectation of obtaining the full point.

4) Tell your opponent to call in the controller if he wishes, but mate by a legal move ends the game and that is it!

5) Write down any move other than 111 ♖xd3+ and claim a draw under the fifty-move rule. It is unfortunate for Black that he would have had mate next move!

6) Restart his clock and, as a sign of goodwill, offer your scoresheet for him to bring his up to date. After he has done this, he can then restart your clock.

Faulty Tactics

1) Baker – G. Morris
Cardiff 1998

The rook sacrifice is correct.

22 ♖xe6+! fxe6 23 ♕xe6+ ♕e7 24 ♖e1! ♕xe6 25 ♖xe6+ ♔d7 26 ♔xg2 h6 27 ♖xf6 hxg5 28 ♖xb6

White has a convincing material and positional advantage. The game concluded:

28...♖hb8 29 ♘d5 ♔d8 30 ♖g6 1-0

However, White had no need to sacrifice, as 22 ♕f5! wins easily.

2) Machulsky – M. Pavlović
Belgrade 1998

28...♖xd4??

After 28...♖h8 Black still has a small edge.

29 f4

Now White's e-pawn is no longer pinned.

29...♕h6 30 ♖h1

Winning material while avoiding any counterplay after 30 exd4 ♖h8.

30...♕xh1+ 31 ♔xh1

Black could now have resigned.

3) Steele – Baker
Cardiff 1998

16 ♘xf6+?!

16 ♗a2 b3 is good for Black but not conclusive.

16...♕xf6! 17 ♗g5 ♘xf3!

Not 17...♘d3+?? 18 cxd3 ♕xb2+ 19 ♕xb2 ♗xb2+ 20 ♔xb2 bxa3+ 21 ♔xa3 axb3+ 22 ♔xb3 ♗a4+ 23 ♔c4

♗xd1 24 ♖xd1, when White has a decisive advantage.

18 ♗xf6 ♘xd2 19 ♗d5 ♗xf6 20 ♗xa8 ♗xb2+! 21 ♔xb2 ♘c4+ 22 ♔a2 ♖xa8 23 axb4 ♘e3

Black is very well placed.

4) Agdestein – de Firmian
Reykjavik 1998

52...♕xf3+!!

An attractive simplifying combination.

53 ♕xf3 ♗xf3 54 gxf7+ ♔xf7 55 ♔xf3

This brings about an ending with an unusual material distribution, in which White puts up an imaginative but ultimately hopeless defence.

55...a4

White is unable to stop the a-pawn, so instead he makes a bold attempt to set up a fortress.

56 h5 a3 57 ♗xe6+ ♔g7 58 ♔e4 a2 59 ♔d5 a1♕ 60 ♔d6 ♕a7 61 ♔c6 ♔f8 62 h6 ♕h7 63 ♗d5 ♕xh6+ 64 e6 ♔e7 65 ♔xb6

It might seem that White has set up an impregnable fortress. All the white pieces are protected, and the black king cannot approach his counterpart. However...

65...♔d6 66 ♔a6 ♕g7 67 b6 ♕a1+ 68 ♔b7 ♕a4 69 ♔b8 ♕a6 70 b7 ♕b6

Zugzwang!

71 ♗e4 ♔xe6 72 ♔c8 ♕a6 73 ♗f3 ♔e7 74 ♗d5 ♕d6 75 b8♘

75 b8♕ ♕d7#.

75...♕b6 0-1

Due to the killing threat of ...♔d6 and ...♕c7.

5) Zaja – Sale
Croatian Ch 1998

19 ♘h6+!! gxh6 20 ♗xh6 ♖e5

After 20...♔e7, 21 ♖ae1+ ♔d7 22 ♗xf8 ends Black's resistance.

21 ♕g7+ ♔e8 22 ♕xf8+ ♔d7 23 ♗f4

White has regained the material invested but maintains all of the attacking chances while Black remains bottled up on the queenside.

6) A. Richardson – Baker
Hanham 1998

17 ♕xe5?? ♕f8!

Now g7 is protected while the queen on e5 is attacked and has no retreat to protect the bishop on b2.

18 ♕xg7+ ♕xg7 19 ♗xg7 ♔xg7

The rest is just technique.

7) Volzhin – Baker
Hastings Challengers 1997/8

14...c5??

Now, too late, Black saw that after 15 dxc5 ♗xc5 that White would win a piece with the simple 16 ♖e5.

8) Kramnik – Ivanchuk
Linares 1998

In fact, this is a very good question! In the game, White played the 'safe' 13 ♖b3 and the game was drawn in 58 moves. Anand though, who was passing the board at the time, was fascinated by the following possibility:

13 ♕g3!?

Anand: "A rook sacrifice of great creativity." This move leads to extremely complex positions with the basic idea of White attempting to mate Black quickly on g7.

13...♕xc3+ 14 ♔d1 g6 15 ♕g5 ♕a1+

15...♕b2 16 ♗d3 ♕c3 17 ♔e2 dxc4 18 ♗e4 ♕a5 19 d5 and Black is struggling to stop the threat of ♕h6, while 15...♘b4 allows 16 g4! ♘d3 17 ♗xd3 ♕xd3+ 18 ♔e1 and again Black cannot stop the mating threat.

16 ♔e2 ♕b1! 17 g4 ♕e4 18 ♔d2

Now:

a) 18...♕f3?? loses to 19 ♗e2.

b) 18...♘xd4! 19 exd4 e5! 20 ♕e3 ♕b1! (20...♕xe3+ 21 fxe3 exd4 22 exd4 dxc4 23 ♗xc4 and the strength of the bishop-pair offers White the better chances) 21 ♕h6 and Black must take the perpetual check by 21...♕b2+ 22 ♔e1 ♕b1+, etc., which White has no good way to avoid.

Bolts from the Blue

1) Timman – Short
Tilburg 1990

1 ♕c4+! ♔h8 2 ♘f7+ ♔g8 3 ♘h6++ ♔h8 4 ♕g8+! ♖xg8 5 ♘f7# (1-0)

2) Bolt – Baker
Monmouth 1997

21...♗g4 0-1

Due to 22 ♕xg4 ♕xe3+ 23 ♔f1 ♕f2#.

3) Gershon – Vaïsser
New York 1998

35...♗xg3+!! 0-1
36 ♔xg3 (36 fxg3 ♕c2+ 37 ♔h3 ♕g2+ 38 ♔h4 ♕h2#) 36...♕g1+ 37 ♔xf3 (37 ♔h3 ♕g2+ 38 ♔h4 ♕g4#) 37...♕g4#.

4) Lasker – Steinitz
St Petersburg 1895/6

1 ♕xf4!! exf4 2 ♘f6!
The black queen has no good square to defend against 3 ♘f7#.
2...♘e6
2...♕b5? 3 ♘f7#.
3 ♘xd7
White has a decisive material plus.

5) Botvinnik – Keres
USSR Cht (Moscow) 1966

1 ♖b8!! 1-0
Due to 1...♕xb8 2 ♕xh4 mating.

6) Kasparov – Browne
Banja Luka 1979

1 ♗h7+! ♔xh7
1...♔f8 2 ♕h8#.
2 ♕xe6 1-0
Black cannot avoid the fatal penetration via f7.

7) Alekhine – Shishkov
1919

1 ♖xf2!
White takes the risk! 1 ♖a1? is obviously wrong due to 1...f4 2 a6 f3 3 ♖g1 fxg2+ 4 ♖xg2 ♕f1+ 5 ♖g1 ♕h3#. However, 1 ♖xf5 may transpose to the game after 1...♔xf5 but the text-move is more forcing and avoids Black struggling on with 1...♕d4.
1...gxf2 2 ♖xf5!
This move decoys the black king to a bad square.
2...♔xf5 3 g4+!
This sacrifice clears the g2-square for the white king.
3...♔xg4 4 ♔g2 1-0
The a-pawn queens.

8) Stamma

1 ♕f4+! gxf4 2 ♗xf4+ ♔a8 3 ♘b6+! axb6 4 axb6+ ♘a6 5 ♖xc8+! ♖xc8 6 ♖xa6+!! bxa6 7 ♗g2+ ♖c6 8 ♗xc6#

9) Tal – Platonov
Dubna 1973

1 ♕h6 ♖xg3 2 ♗g6!! 1-0
As 2...♖xg6 3 fxg6 fxg6 4 ♕xf8# is mate.

10) Ferran – Parra Cabrera
Cuba 1996

1...♗a3! 2 c3!
2 bxa3?? ♕a1#.
2...♘a4!! 3 ♗xa4
3 bxa3 ♘xc3 will soon lead to mate.
3...♕xa4 4 ♗g5 ♖xd1+ 5 ♕xd1 ♗xb2+! 6 ♔d2 ♗xc3+ 7 ♔e2 ♖e8+ 8 ♗e3 ♕c4+ 0-1
It is no longer possible for White to avoid mate.

11) Tal – Olafsson
Las Palmas 1975

1...Qf4!!

Black sacrifices his queen to un-protect the d1-square.

2 Re7!

White counterattacks the defender of rook on d8. Obviously, 2 Qxf4 Rd1+ 3 Ne1 Rxe1# is unacceptable.

2...Rf8

Now the defender of the first rank is really attacked. Instead, 2...Rxd2 3 Rxe8+ Kg7 4 Nxd2 gives White has a decisive material advantage, while after 2...Qxd2 the intermediary capture with check, 3 Rxe8+, leaves White with all the chances after 3...Rxe8 4 Nxd2.

3 Qa5

After 3 Qe1 Bxf3 4 gxf3 Qg5+ White loses a rook, while 3 Qe2 Bxf3 4 Qxf3 Qd6 gives Black a double threat against the rook on e7 and back-rank mate.

3...Rd1+ 4 Ne1 Qg5!

A further queen sacrifice attacks the defender of the e1-knight.

5 Qb4 Qxe7 0-1

12) Topalov – Shirov
Linares 1998

47...Bh3!!

The key to Black's winning plan is to advance his a- and d-pawns as quickly as possible. He also needs to bring his king up, via f5 and e4, to support them without any delay. He therefore needs to move his bishop so as to attack something. Putting it on e4 doesn't solve the puzzle, because although White would need to lose time defending his g2-pawn (or keeping it defended), the black king would be denied access to the e4-square. The 'logical' move is to put the bishop on h3. Here it does not obstruct the king, and it does attack the g2-pawn, but there is the small matter of it being *en prise* on this square! However, the loss of the bishop turns out to be less important than the activity of the black king and pawns – Black can win the ending a piece down.

Making Shirov's move all the more amazing, it also seems that it was necessary. There is no clear way forward for Black after either 47...a3 48 Kf2 a2 49 Ke3 Bg4 50 g3 Kf5 51 Bd4 or 47...Be4 48 Kf2 Kf5 49 g3.

48 gxh3

After 48 Kf2 Kf5 49 Kf3 Bxg2+ 50 Kxg2 Ke4 51 Bxf6 d4 52 Be7 Kd3 53 Kf2 Kc2 54 Bb4 d3 Black wins, e.g. 55 Ke1 a3! 56 Bxa3 d2+ and the d-pawn queens.

48...Kf5 49 Kf2 Ke4 50 Bxf6

Or 50 Ke2 a3 51 Kd2 d4 52 Ba1 f5 and the white king and bishop are unable to stop all the pawns.

50...d4 51 Be7

Or 51 Ke2? a3 and the a-pawn queens.

51...Kd3! 52 Bc5 Kc4 53 Be7

53 Bxd4 Kxd4 54 Ke2 Kc3 55 Kd1 Kb2 guides the black a-pawn home.

53...Kb3 0-1

White resigned due to 54 Bc5 d3 55 Ke3 Kc2 56 Bb4 a3, when one of the black pawns will promote.

Conclusion

One important subject has only been touched upon lightly in this book: motivation. We each have our own reasons for wanting to play chess, and to improve our game, but it is all too easy, especially for young players, to lose interest or to become jaded.

I therefore believe it is vital for a coach to make sure their pupils feel inspired, are given realistic goals, and are immersed in the right culture for them to enjoy playing and learning. With that in mind, I include some 'fun' sections during a group coaching session. During this I may show them how even very strong players can make the most awful and basic of errors. I include in this one of my own horrors from years ago when I lost as White to Bernard Cafferty as follows: 1 e4 ♘f6 2 ♘c3 d5 3 e5 ♘e4!? 4 ♘ce2 ♘c5 5 c3?? ♘d3#. Moreover, I relate the story behind this game and not only its importance to me at the time but also its psychological effect on me. Events like that can hurt a player and even encourage him to give up chess. However, if the player is strong-willed enough, it can make him stronger and even more determined. The ability to laugh at oneself in such circumstances should not be underestimated.

Sometimes people around a young player, and by that I mean parents, coaches, clubmates, etc., lose sight of something very basic - if the child doesn't enjoy what he is doing, then he will find something else to do instead! A child's involvement in chess may be based on various factors, e.g. parental influence, curiosity, a tendency towards intellectual pursuits or an enthusiastic chess teacher at school. Whatever causes children to take up chess, the motivation may not be strong to start with, and therefore their interest needs to be nurtured and their participation encouraged as much as possible.

I hope that there is much of this book that the reader will find interesting, useful and thought-provoking. It is my own belief that to improve we must first look very much to ourselves as much as trying to learn from others.

Index of Players

Numbers refer to pages. When a page reference appears in **bold**, the named player had White.

Index of Openings

Numbers refer to pages.